OTHER BOOKS BY THE AUTHOR
The Violent Gang
Synanon: The Tunnel Back
The Hippie Trip
Robopaths: People as Machines
Crime and Delinquency (with Martin Haskell)
Criminology: Crime and Criminality (with Martin Haskell)
Juvenile Delinquency (with Martin Haskell)
George Raft
Psychodrama: Resolving Emotional Problems Through Role-Playing
The Extra-Sex Factor
The Little League Game (with Jon Brower)

FATHERS
AND SONS

Lewis Yablonsky, Ph.D.

Simon and Schuster • New York

LIBRARY OF CONGRESS CATALOGING IN PUBLICATION DATA

YABLONSKY, LEWIS.
FATHERS AND SONS.

INCLUDES BIBLIOGRAPHICAL REFERENCES.
1. FATHERS.   2. FATHERS AND SONS.
HQ756.Y3   306.8'7   81-21524
AACR2
ISBN 0-671-25461-8

*For my father, Harry
and my son, Mitch*

CONTENTS

PREFACE

EVERY PERSON WOULD like to have an ideal father, a superman who would soothe his life by helping him solve his problems and give crystal-clear logical directions for attaining a state of emotional nirvana and success. In a utopian society where everyone would have a perfect father who fulfilled all of these idealized expectations, there would be no social problems. A superfather would solve all personal problems, and this would automatically contribute to the amelioration and control of violence, depression, mental illness, war and crime in the overall society.

An important lifelong bond between fathers and sons is forged at birth. There is enormous evidence of this cohesive force, and it totally contradicts the myths perpetuated by some that men are less emotional, less caring, less involved, less loving than women are toward their children. My data, based on in-depth and survey interviews with hundreds of fathers and sons, support the fact that almost all men have profound positive emotions about their sons. I am convinced by my research that the so-called "maternal instinct" attributed to women exists in a parallel form in men as a "paternal instinct."

Because of this intense involvement, the formation of every man's basic personality is significantly influenced by his father. The complexity of the personality formation process, the interactions that take place, the expectation father and son have of each other, produce great emotional satisfaction as well as conflict. The fact that fathers and sons have deep, often lifelong struggles with each other is more of a testimonial to their feelings about each other than proof of a lack of caring. Basic conflicts often emerge when a father perceives his son's behavior as self-defeating. In his caring effort to set his son straight, the father

9

often incites a normal rebellion. A greater awareness of these normal conflicts by both fathers and sons can minimize the negative consequences.

A basic goal of this analysis is to illuminate these conflicts, normal and abnormal, for the purpose of redirecting the amount of energy wasted on useless struggles between father and son. Getting their basic relationship on track and in synchronization can eliminate a considerable amount of wasteful emotional problems that tend to negatively affect family life and the larger society. A better understanding of the father-son relationship is of primary importance to men because they live these roles. The subject, however, is of equal importance to women, especially mothers, because they are central figures in the dramatic scenarios between fathers and sons, and the quality of their lives is crucially affected by the fathers and sons in their families.

As a sociologist, I considered myself an expert on the socialization of children and the fathering process, until my son was born. At that point in my life, I realized how little I really knew. The fact that I have a son was, therefore, no small factor in my motivation to carry out this study. My enormous feelings of love for my son and my desire to bring him up properly motivated me to study the process. In researching this book, therefore, my relationship with my son was of enormous importance. He taught me a great deal about the dynamics of fathering during the critical years from birth to his current age of eighteen.

Over the past four years, I have carried out two types of research into the subject of fathers and sons. One approach involved *in-depth interviews* with over one hundred men about their dual roles of father and son. The second type, the *research survey method*, involved a comprehensive questionnaire that was administered to 564 men covering a range of socioeconomic positions in our society.

Beyond this direct research, my clinical experiences over the past thirty years as a research professor of sociology, group psychotherapist and psychodramatist have contributed greatly to my comprehension of the emotional relationship of fathers and sons. In particular, my work in psychodrama and group psychotherapy, which involved my directing several thousand sessions concerned with the specific problems of fathers and sons from all walks of life, has contributed to my understanding of the subject. All of my findings from these various research sources, both professional and personal, are woven into the book.

I am grateful to my son, Mitch, who endured the burden of these research years with style and grace, and has emerged a solid man. My brothers Morris and Joe dug deep into their psyches to reveal fascinating material about my father and our early family situation. My friends and colleagues, Cathy Apstein, Norman Herman, Ben Krentzman, Marshall Cherkes, Al Pierce, Howard Sackler and Mike Soloman, freely shared with me their own life experiences and insights into the subject.

I am especially grateful to my dear friend and colleague, Dr. George Bach, who contributed enormously to the book's content with his theories and case material.

Lewis Yablonsky, Ph.D.
Department of Sociology
California State University
Northridge, California

CHAPTER ONE

The Father's Role: Dreams and Messages

THE MOST IMPORTANT role a man can play in his lifetime is that of becoming a father. Fatherhood is a man's link with the future. His progeny carries his name and inherits his social, emotional and financial legacy. Even if a son rebels against the philosophical message his father delivers to him on how to live his life, he is enormously affected by his father.

Men like John F. Kennedy and Martin Luther King, who had profound and positive influences on our society, were enormously affected by their fathers. In contrast, a case can be made for the fact that tyrannical mass murderers like Adolf Hitler or Charles Manson might well have led humanistic lives if they had had effective, caring fathers. These are special dramatic cases; however, every man is significantly influenced by his father.

A shift toward a more positive, intelligent enactment of the father role would affect the overall society. More effective fathering could virtually eliminate such social problems as crime, drug abuse and the violence that plagues our society.

Although sex roles are changing, fathers, because they are more likely than mothers to be involved with the larger society, are the primary transmitters of the basic rules of the society to their sons. Due to this fact, they have a profound influence on how their sons live their lives.

Boys tend to be heavily involved emotionally with their fathers as role models, even though they may spend more time with their mothers, sisters and peers. Boys look to their fathers for cues as to how to act out their male roles, and specifically, later on, their roles as fathers.

Sons strongly indentify with their fathers and believe they will have many of the same experiences as their fathers. For example, in a group therapy session I directed, a man revealed how as a child he was always concerned with his father's physical health because he believed on a deep emotional level that he would have all of the maladies of his father when he became a man. To reinforce this assumption about sons identifying with their fathers, I have noted in my research that, curiously, many sons expect to live about as long as their fathers. Specifically, some men become pathologically depressed when they approach the exact age at which their fathers died. There is, of course, some basis in medical research that reveals that the degree of longevity is inherited, but most of these feelings are emotionally based.

In general, the amount of contact between fathers and sons determines the degree to which their personalities are enmeshed with each other from the son's birth. For most fathers, an infant son is an ego extension, and this feeling persists at least until the teenage years. A son's successes and defeats are felt deeply by the father. In this regard, sports activities can be as revealing as a Rorschach test in evaluating father-son relationships. Some fathers use sports to solidify the sons' roles as ego extensions. For this type of father, the sport becomes a kind of psychodrama in which he lives out his own need to win in life through his son, and any rejection the son experiences is personalized by the father. As one father said in a psychological slip to a little league coach who had benched his son, "You can't do this to me."

The intense and mixed emotions that flare in some fathers about the way their ego-extension sons are treated were reported to me by one little league father, a man in his forties. His point of view in the following scenario reveals the intensity of a father's emotional involvement with his eight-year-old son, and how their egos often merge.

"I consider myself to be an urbane, intelligent and compassionate man. For the first time in over thirty years I was about to become physically violent—I was ready to punch my son's coach in the mouth.

"The incident arose with my arrival at the field in the waning innings of the game to find my son not pitching his team and his father to glory. I found him in the stands with angry tears in his eyes, with his mother trying to calm him down. 'What happened?'

"The story I got was that the manager had expelled him from the field and even the dugout because he had asked once too often to get into the game. I controlled myself until the last pitch of the game was tossed. The manager had delivered his usual diatribe in the dugout about their terrible loss, how they were all babies and rotten ballplayers.

"I approached him when he was alone out of a sincere desire to understand the severity of my son's crime. Had he really deserved excommunication and humiliation in front of his teammates and a baseball stand full of parents and fans?

"He told me that he had warned my son that if he asked once more to get into the game he was *out*. I mumbled something about my understanding of the need for discipline with nine- and ten-year-olds, but that I thought his actions were a little harsh. After all, all my son wanted to do was play ball.

"He then proceeded to tell me what a lousy father I was, that my kid was spoiled and immature, and that if I didn't knock it off, he was personally going to throw my son out of the league. I said, 'You can't say that about Bill' [and me]. As we stood practically jaw to jaw, he replied, 'One more word out of your mouth and you're both out of this league for good.'

"It was at this point that I was prepared, at a minimum, to knock the creep down. Several people intervened. He backed off and so did I. A state of détente was arranged and my son finished the season, but I seethe every time I think of that son-of-a-bitch coach and how he treated us."

The incident reveals the degree of ego-merging that often exists between a father and his son during the early years of their relationship. In time, when the son reaches adolescence, the father's place in his son's life begins to change as the son seeks his own identity. This process of normal separation from the father often involves battles for position and control. The normal struggle between a father and son as a result of the son's efforts to become "his own man" (even when he's not ready for the responsibility) can be minimized when the father is aware of the dynamics.

The struggle sometimes takes place over absurd issues. As a case in point, in a psychodrama I ran with a teenager whose father was a nationally known writer, the following ridiculous dialogue developed.

FATHER (looking at an essay written by his son for school): Son, this is a fine piece of work, but there are a few grammatical errors . . .

SON: Oh, bullshit! What do you know about writing? I'll ask my teacher.

The father reacted emotionally and indignantly to this put-down. How could a high school English teacher know more about writing than he did? He, of course, had missed the point of his son's reaction, which had little to do with writing. The son was overreacting to the feeling of contrast with his father, and the feeling that he could *never* write as well as his father. Any reminder of his feelings, including his father's well-intentioned corrections, infuriated the son.

In another role-playing scene, the sight of one of the father's books produced intense negative emotions in the son. In this session, the father was made aware of his son's emotional reaction to the book, and how his son was overwhelmed by his feeling that writing even one page was terribly difficult. When the boy made an unconscious comparison between a few pages of his schoolwork and an entire book by his father, he was overwhelmed. After several counseling sessions on the conflict between him and his son, the father became aware of his son's perspective on writing and the disparity between the son's writing and the father's writing at that period in their respective lives. As a result of his insight he took the time to work patiently with his son on the matter. His son responded to this special attention and began to see that in his own context, compared to his peers (not his father), he was doing very well. The son was also appropriately assured by his father that in the course of his own natural development he would at some future time probably begin to write as well as his father, if that became his goal in life.

An important factor which emerges during these early years

is the impact a son has on his father and on the father's various roles in society. Fathers, if they listen carefully, can learn a great deal from their sons. Extending the Wordsworth poetic theme, "The child is father of the Man," my research reveals that fathers are heavily affected by their sons. One man, a psychologist, told me, "I already had my Ph.D. and was a practicing psychologist when my son was born. I thought I knew a lot about the socialization process and human behavior from my lifelong study of the subject. But I think I learned more about human behavior from watching my son develop in his first ten years than I ever learned at any university. I always was aware of how fathers affected their sons, but I am increasingly conscious of the enormous impact sons can have on how their fathers live out their lives."

In enacting the father role, some formerly cold, even psychopathic, men become compassionate and empathetic toward their sons in a way that has a positive effect on how they treat people in general. In other cases, men become good loving fathers but maintain a negative role in the world at large.

In Geoffrey Wolff's autobiography *The Duke of Deception*, in effect a lengthy case history of a father-son relationship, the author reveals how his father was paradoxically "a bad man but a good father." On his father's death he wrote:

I had felt betrayed by my father and wanted to betray him. . . . He had never repudiated me or seen in my face intimations of his own mortality. He had never let me think he wished to be rid of me or the burden of my judgment, even when I had hounded him about his history, had quibbled with its details like a small-print artist, like a reviewer, for God's sake! He didn't try to form me in his own image. How could he? Which image to choose? He had wanted me to be happier than he had been, to do better. He had taught me many things, some of which were important, some of which he meant, some of which were true. The things he told me were the right things to tell a son, usually, and by the time I understood their source in mendacity they had done what good they could. I had been estranged from my father by my apprehension of other people's opinion of him, and by a compulsion to be free of his chaos and destructions. I had forgotten I loved him mostly, and mostly now I missed him. I miss him.[1]

Wolff's father was a con man who let his family and son down more often than not. Most details of his father's life story reveal him as a blatant psychopath, a pathological liar, a cheat not to be trusted; yet in his own way he effectively played his role of father. Wolff knew that his father, who was gone a great deal, would somehow materialize when he needed him. He relates many incidents which reveal how his father would appear and invariably help him solve critical problems in his life. His father gave him a positive message and was there for him when he needed him, despite the fact that he himself was a failure in life.

A prominent psychiatrist I've known over the years had the opposite effect on his son. Unlike Wolff's father, who was a psychopath and a liar, the psychiatrist was a brilliant therapist, very knowledgeable about proper theories of child rearing and, in fact, a wonderful man. Yet he was a failure in the role of father. His son turned out badly, turning to drugs and crime partly because his father could not utilize his vast knowledge of proper child rearing to help his son to grow up effectively.

Knowledge and skill about the fathering process may be valuable, but they don't insure positive results in the socialization and development of a son, unless they are somehow integrated into the father-son relationship. Wolff's father, despite his negative worldly role, cared about his son and instinctively acted in an effective fashion. The psychiatrist, with all his training, was not able to utilize his vast knowledge of human behavior to father his son properly.

As a sociologist and group therapist I considered myself something of an expert on how a child's personality is formed by his social context and his parents. I rapidly found out that my professional background was of limited value in socializing my son. I enacted my father role, in concert with my wife, mainly based on my emotional feelings about my son.

During my wife's pregnancy, and especially at my son's birth (March 4th, 1964), I had feelings which I had never previously experienced. For the first time in my life I felt a love that had no

18

boundaries. The baby boy I saw wheeled out by the nurse the night he was born was, I felt, clearly entitled to everything I had. My love for him wás unlike any other love I'd felt for any other person. It was boundless, joyful and unconditional.

For the first six euphoric months, my basic reasoning powers and training in human behavior were almost totally divorced from my responses to him. His joy was my joy. His pain or discomfort was mine. It was as if I were his double, experiencing his emotions as fully and effortlcssly as possible.

His mother was a colleague in rearing the child who became the centerpiece of both of our lives. There was seldom any father-mother, male-female division of labor. His basic needs were our needs, and we both administered the fundamental care, foods, playfulness and emotional responses we felt were so necessary for his sustenance, growth and development.

When he was about two years old, certain objective realities began to intrude on my idyllic and beautiful symbiotic relationship with my son. I became aware of the logical reality that I had to give him more room to explore life on his own without my constant presence as his guide. Life for him now presented certain potential hazards such as hot stoves, open doors, street traffic and an occasional disagreeable stranger. There were peers who didn't always respond to him with the same affection that flowed from his parents.

A certain element of fear on my part crept into our relationship. As he began to emerge physically from three to around ten, I no longer had complete control over his comfort and safety. Moreover, I knew there were certain situations he had to confront if he were to mature and be able to handle life on his own. I became increasingly aware of the fundamental and logical reality that if I continued for much longer to treat him as lovingly, and perhaps smotheringly, as when he was younger, I would be doing him an enormous disservice.

It was at around that time that I began to think more about *him* than *us*. Obviously, if he were to live effectively in the world, *he* had to begin to confront some societal realities, issues and problems in his own way. A large amount of my anxiety stemmed from the certainty that he would be increasingly on his own, and that I would at some point be useless to him in confronting issues and relationships, especially potentially harmful ones. He must eventually be able to confront life forcefully and effectively on his own.

This fact of life sets up a normal tug-of-war between an *involved* (perhaps overinvolved) father and his son. How much should the son be permitted to be on his own? To what extent should the father, in performing his role, let his son fight his own battles with his peers, and when should he interfere? When does schoolwork become the exclusive responsibility of the son, an arena in which he must succeed or fail on his own?

Basically, in a healthy parent-child relationship there are increments of freedom granted to the child which correspond to the child's ability to function independently. As Erich Fromm points out in his profound book *Escape From Freedom*, with each measure of freedom a person obtains there are concomitant dimensions of responsibility to be assumed. According to Fromm some people never learn how to handle freedom, and therefore live out their lives in symbiotic dependency relationships.

There were many milestones in our father-son relationship in terms of this letting-go process with my son. It is my view that there is a slowly unfolding process of increasing freedom from infancy to eleven or twelve, and the most pronounced delineation takes place around the time a boy enters adolescence.

The almost absurd degree to which I had *doubled* for my son —to which my ego was merged with his—during the early years of our relationship was revealed to me on one occasion when we were driving to the ball field. He was scheduled to pitch a championship baseball game. As I drove, I actually began to think to myself how tired *I* was, and I thought, I simply didn't want to pitch today. My other, more rational, self turned on this doubling idiot inside me and said, "You're not pitching today—*he* is." That incident revealed to me the almost pathologically overinvolved relationship I had with my son, and the fact that the time had clearly come when it was necessary for our egos to cleanly separate. Interestingly, it was my son, not I, who finally clarified the separation.

He was thirteen at the time, and had played five seasons. Mitch was a better than average player, and I had high hopes that he would continue to experience the game and its joys as I had, perhaps on through high school or beyond. He wanted to quit the league at midseason for what appeared to me to be no reason. We had several critical encounters which would end up with him crying and me yelling at him to not become a quitter. "You owe it to your team to not quit in midseason!" (I never gave him the real underlying message, which I now know was, "Do it for me. I love reliving those happy years I had playing ball around that age. It was the only activity I shared with my father. And it was the main activity in my life for which he gave me approval. Please don't quit the team. You're potentially a better player than I. And maybe you'll fulfill my unrealized dream of playing in the big leagues. Through you I have a second chance at baseball stardom.")

A key situation then took place between my son and me before one ball game. He had put on his uniform, and we continued our argument about his finishing the season. Finally he screamed at me in a loud voice in front of a stand full of fans and parents, "*It's your fucking league, not mine.*"

I was hurt and furious at the time, but later, after quiet contemplation, I realized the degree to which I was personally involved, doubling for him and controlling his life as I had done during his infancy and early childhood. He saw this negative symbiosis between us more clearly than I, and this incident revealed to me his normal adolescent need to separate from me and be on his own. Quitting the league was one step on his part toward fulfilling this need.

This brief example reveals several general aspects of our father-son relationship at that time. One is the transition of my concept of "we" to "he and I" that had to transpire for him to move naturally out of his childhood period into his teenage years; and secondly, the necessity for correcting my pattern of overwhelming him by acting as if "his league"—his problems—were always mine. The separation of our identities was vital to both of us in defining our relationship through the teenage years, and to developing the significant friendship that has emerged in his early adult years. Despite our normal conflicts, my loving-doubling approach with my son had been effective and functional up to his teenage years. At that point in time it was no longer in proper synchronization with his needs or mine. The role a father should properly enact with his son goes through several phases of change.

Mothers still predominate as the closer, more outwardly emotional, nurturing parent in a child's socialization, but men, especially young men, are increasingly carrying out at least half of all the responsibilities of parenting. In contemporary society we are moving closer toward androgynous roles to the point where those of the mother and father may someday be totally interchangeable in the pre-teen years.

The role of the father has changed dramatically in the past century, partly as a result of the movement of a large part of the population from a rural to a more urban technological lifestyle, and partly because of the changing roles of men and women in contemporary society. In the rural setting the father role entailed being a more distant "head of the family," who was the top manager of the social and economic functioning of the family. Also, in simpler societies, children, especially sons, were more likely to make valuable contributions to the family's social and economic life.

Less complex societies produced a more functional relationship between fathers and sons than today's urban-technological system. A father had a special importance in such social systems, because he served as a direct role model for his son. In such societies the father could help his son by showing him specific ways to earn his living, and in response the son at some point became a significant contributer to his father and the family. There is a wealth of anthropological case material which describes this more functional father-son relationship. For example, a father in New Guinea comments on his relationship to his son as follows: ". . . when Marigum was making a new canoe he allowed his youngest son, Sabawaki, to take an axe and chip at the dugout. On my inquiring whether the boy did not impede his progress the father agreed that he would be able to work much faster alone. 'But if I send the child away,' he added, 'how can I expect him to know anything? This time he was in the way, but I'm showing him, and when we have to make another canoe he'll be really useful.' "[2]

Regrettably, there are few real situations in contemporary society for fathers and sons to *functionally* relate in basic ways. The demise of family small businesses and artisan apprenticeships has left a functional vacuum.

In contemporary society fathers construct relatively artificial activities to fill the vacuum. These include vacation trips, camping and sports. In situations where a father and son go off on a camping trip, there may be real camaraderie and meaningful interaction; however, these are relatively artificial situations when compared to farm life or the tribal situation where a father and son literally hunted for their family's food supply. In these situations their activities may have been recreational, but were also vitally functional, and both father and son were more dynamically related to each other and their family.

Because of contemporary technological society's complicated divisions of labor, there is usually greater alienation between father and son. In today's society, fathers and sons have less to share with each other in the day-to-day living process.

Because of these vital changes, it is increasingly important to nourish the emotional relationship between fathers and sons. Fathers need to break away from the macho unemotional facade in enacting the father role, and should become loving-doubling fathers who openly demonstrate their deeper feelings for their sons. This is required as compensation for the lack of the more natural relationship context of the past.

Apart from the technological impacts cited, another factor that has affected the traditional roles of fathers and mothers in recent years in the movement toward greater equality between men and women. The effects of this social movement have been felt in the home and in the larger society. The movement has resulted in more and more women entering and attaining status and power in occupations which were formerly the exclusive province of men. As more and more women move out of the home into the work force, fathers are called upon to fill the vacuum by assuming roles and functions formerly dominated by wives in the traditional role of mother.

23

Because of this social change in sex roles, the traditional role of the mother has undergone dramatic changes. Most working mothers trying to succeed in the job market have less time to perform the traditional mother role. In the 1980s many of the processes of intense emotional nurturing formerly almost the exclusive province of mothers, have become part of the role performed by modern fathers.

In her book *My Mother/My Self*, Nancy Friday agrees with my viewpoint and aptly points out that profound changes in father and mother roles must take place if the women's movement is to succeed:

> Women who want to be able to experience the alternatives and options necessary to grow in our complex society must accept that both men and women have the desire and capability to take care of babies. . . . A lot of people, and this includes men, do like to take care of small, dependent people. . . . I've come to believe what is ordinarily called the "maternal instinct" is just this simple liking "to take care of" smaller creatures. Some human beings do not like it at all. It is not some great biological imperative, which if frustrated will ruin or impoverish a woman's life. . . . Men were born with about the same capacity as women to care for and nurture children —except for the obvious biological differences. . . . The most direct way for women to do that is to realize that any human can parent small children. Acceptance and the encouragement of men as this type of nurturing father would free women to explore other powers they have.[3]

The traditional male-female father-mother roles have undergone vast changes in the past decades. What has surfaced in recent years is the obvious desire of many women to enact what has traditionally been the male role of moving out of the home into the world of employment in society. (More than 50 percent of married women today are employed outside the home.) Also in accordance with this trend of changing sex roles, many men have abandoned their former macho distant-father postures which basically involved providing food, clothes and shelter for the family, and have begun to openly love and nurture their children in ways traditionally ascribed to mothers. There is increasing evidence that men can function in the loving-doubling father role as effectively as women do in the traditional mother role.

Men can enlarge their human experience by providing basic care for infants and children. Through feeding them when they are hungry, changing diapers when necessary and dealing with their emotional needs, a man can learn a great deal more about the human condition. Men who relate to their children in this more complete way generally develop the ability to be more compassionate and humanistic in all of their relationships in life.

Research evidence from cross-cultural, historical, medical and biological sources indicates that fathers are capable of playing an active role in infant development. My research supports the evidence that more fathers are taking this traditional motherly nurturing role seriously, and are becoming more openly emotionally involved with their children.

A series of observational studies of father-infant interaction in a hospital indicated that fathers were as interested and involved with newborn infants and as nurturant as mothers in their interactions with their infants. While mothers spent more time than fathers in feeding and care-taking activities, fathers and mothers did not differ in their care-taking competence as revealed by their sensitivity to infant cues in feeding situations. The following series of statements summarizes the current research findings on the father's role during the child's infancy: (1) fathers are interested in newborns and, if provided with the opportunity, become very involved; (2) fathers are just as nurturant as mothers in their interactions with newborns; (3) fathers do apparently engage in less care-taking, but; (4) when offered the opportunity, fathers can be capable and competent in the execution of care-taking activities.

In summary, in our society of changing sex roles, many more women are moving toward reducing the amount of time and energy they have devoted to their mothering roles in the direction of entering occupational and other areas that have been predominantly the male province. As this takes place, the fathering role becomes increasingly significant in influencing a male child's personality. With mothers working more and more by choice, fathers must be prepared to fill the vacuum created by

25

working wives. From the evidence of research and from my own interviews and observations, it is clear to me that changing sex roles have already produced fathers who "mother," and mothers who "father." In fact, we would do well to recognize clearly that such traits as the ability to love compassionately and to nurture exist equally in both men and women. Moreover, the desire of fathers to become more emotionally involved in the lives of their infants should not be interpreted as a threat to the status of mothers. Rather, it means that mothers need no longer bear the sole and, for many, the frightening responsibility for the total rearing of their children. Instead, child-rearing should be seen as a venture in which both parents are jointly engaged. Parental cooperation and mutual participation in child-rearing can also strengthen the marital relationship.

The popularity and success of the Academy Award-winning film *Kramer vs. Kramer* may be due to the film's depiction of some of the potential results of changing father and mother roles in American society. Soon after the film opens, the young mother leaves her husband and son to "find herself." We learn that the husband was, prior to her departure, a traditional father who took financial care of his family, but was away a great deal at his job in advertising, ferociously trying to "make it" in the business world.

After his wife leaves, we see him at first struggling with the necessity of being both mother and father to his son while he maintains his aggressive occupational role. He is awkward at first in relating emotionally to his son, but rapidly and poignantly we witness his loving and compassionate concern for his son emerge in a series of scenes. As his nurturing-father strength develops, we see him becoming increasingly effective at and enjoying his new role. The father's comment from the witness stand during the trial in which his wife attempts to regain custody of their son states the key issue: Who is to say that a mother is a better parent than a father to a young child?

THE MESSAGE

Polonius's message to his son Laertes on his departure to France:

> There—my blessing with thee!
> And these few precepts in thy memory
> Look thou character. Give thy thoughts no tongue,
> Nor any unproportioned thought his act.
> Be thou familiar, but by no means vulgar.
> Those friends thou hast, and their adoption tried,
> Grapple them unto thy soul with hoops of steel,
> But do not dull thy palm with entertainment
> Of each new-hatched, unfledged comrade. Beware
> Of entrance to a quarrel; but being in,
> Bear't that th' opposed may beware of thee.
> Give every man thine ear, but few thy voice;
> Take each man's censure, but reserve thy judgment.
> Costly thy habit as thy purse can buy,
> But not expressed in fancy; rich, not gaudy;
> For the apparel oft proclaims the man,
> And they in France of the best rank and station
> Are most select and generous, chief in that.
> Neither a borrower nor a lender be,
> For loan oft loses both itself and friend,
> And borrowing dulls the edge of husbandry.
> This above all, to thine own self be true,
> And it must follow, as the night the day,
> Thou canst not then be false to any man.
> Farewell. My blessing season this in thee!

Hamlet, *Act I, Scene III*
William Shakespeare

A man in his role of father delivers a basic philosophical message to his son. The message is seldom as formal or precise as Polonius's was in his speech to Laertes, but during their lifetime, if a son listens he will hear some basic theme song from his father on the pitfalls of existence and how he should live his life. Father and son significantly interact with each other around these basic philosophical messages, which may be clearly or abstractly delivered. Sons read these messages, which then affect their lives in happy and fulfilling or depressing and dismal ways.

The messages are sometimes contradicted by the way the father lives his life. "Do as I say, not as I do" is the message, but sons observe and react not only to the verbal message but to the actual behavior of their fathers. When a father who is a businessman gives his son a verbal message to be honest and the son then observes him cheating in business, the son gets the more significant bottom-line message.

A son's level of aspiration in life may be subtly determined through messages conveyed by his father's role and behavior. I'll never forget a scene related to this issue which took place when I was researching a drug rehabilitation center. I was interviewing a man in his forties who had been a heroin addict and in and out of prison most of his life. His nine-year-old son happened to be visiting him that day and was listening to the conversation we were having about his father's life and times. At a certain point the man introduced me to his son, proudly announcing to him that I was a college professor. The boy asked me what a college professor was and what he did. I told him as best I could. The boy looked up at his father and said, "I'm going to college." The father laughed at him and went on to denounce what was from his viewpoint a totally ridiculous idea. He gave his son a clear negative message, not only with his words but through his behavior and position in the world, about his son's "absurd" aspiration. It was certain to affect the child's future.

Fathers seldom give clear messages to their sons. Too often they give coded or double messages. Often a father's deeper expectations for his son are obscured by platitudes like, "I just want him to be happy. He can take any job he wants if he's happy." The medical doctor who told me this was, of course, lying. In a psychodrama session where we probed beneath the surface of his real message to his then fifteen-year-old son, it became quite clear that if his son did not become a doctor like him he would be severely disappointed. When pushed a step deeper into his unconscious in the session, he recited that section of the Hippocratic oath which states: "By precept, lecture and every other mode of instruction, I will impart a knowledge of the [medical] art to my own sons. . . ."

Some sons tend to make assessments about the emotional success or failure of their fathers—and then live their lives in terms of their evaluation. For example, in my research into the counterculture (see my book *The Hippie Trip*, Penguin, 1969), I interviewed one son who was on the scene "exploring" because of his negative perception of his father's emotional success in life. His father gave the appearance of success but the message delivered to his son by his behavior about the quality of his life was dismal.

The interview I had with this young man, standing on a corner in Haight-Ashbury in the late sixties, revealed a prototypical issue between fathers and sons during that period, which resulted in many sons dropping out. He was panhandling at the time, looking quite emaciated and "crashing" in different places each night. I soon determined from our conversation that he came from a wealthy background, and that a simple collect phone call would get him the plane fare back to his affluent parents' home. I asked him why he had dropped out. "Look, my old man is very successful in his business. He earns around 75,000 dollars a year, has the house, the cars, the wife and the kids. But I happen to know his life is miserable in every way and he's unhappy. He followed all the rules and signs set up by his father—my grandfather—along the way. You want to know why I dropped out? Well, I don't want to do all the things he did and wind up like my old man. There must be another way to live and I'm trying to find it. *I don't want to become my father.*"

The success of a father's message toward getting his son to succeed by his standards is directly correlated with the son's belief that his father has achieved a real level of happiness. No matter how much a father verbally harangues a son to follow in his path, it seldom works if the father has failed in his son's eyes. Some fathers, like the hippie case described, become negative role models to their sons. Many young men consciously and clearly rebel against the model of a father whom they perceive as a failure in life in terms of emotional happiness.

Many literary works depict a father's message to his son. Arthur Miller admittedly has written about his own father in many of his works, but especially in his plays *All My Sons* and *Death of a Salesman*. Both of these autobiographical works reveal sons encountering fathers who, early in both plays, idolize their fathers, then later find a fatal flaw or a double message of hypocrisy in their fathers. For example, in Miller's *Death of a Salesman*, one son, Biff, loves his father and makes him his complete idol. He believes in his father's message and projected images of the American Dream of Success. The father's admonition throughout the play is "You can't just be liked by people, you must be well liked." When the teenage son discovers his father in a hotel room with a prostitute, he is disillusioned with him, reacts with bitterness and in effect gives up on life to become a drifter. Toward the end of the play, the father tells his son that he's ruined his life out of spite toward his father. Part of Miller's message in his plays is that when a father and son love each other the father has considerable power over his son. The son believes his father's message, wants to be like his father and fulfill his father's dreams. The son discovers the father's overt message is a fraud when he discovers his father's "feet of clay," and concludes he must develop his own guiding themes in life. My research reveals that this basic dramatic theme is played out between many fathers and sons in real life.

Most sons would like their fathers' messages to be profound, and full of valuable directions on how to live their lives. In many cases, however, there is a point where a son becomes disillusioned with his father's message when he discovers the hypocrisy with which his father really lives his life. It is at that point that a son finds he has to develop his own personal functional guiding themes, or internalize his own message on how to live his life.

A father's message can set his son up to have a self-concept either of failure or success. A physician friend of mine and I were discussing father messages one day, and I asked him what basic message his father had given him. At first he said, "None." After pressing him awhile he said, "Now I have it. My father gave me a clear message that I would fail."

I responded, "Isn't it great that his message didn't affect you?"

The doctor said, "What do you mean?"

"Well, you have not failed."

"What? Yes, I have."

I was quite shocked to hear him say that, because I saw him as a very successful physician who had set up a very effective medical clinic in Venice, California, where he often provided extremely low-cost quality medical care for poor people. From his point of view he had fulfilled his father's prophecy of failure because he wasn't a high-priced Beverly Hills doctor, even though he admitted that he could have been, had that been what he wanted.

My own father, now ninety, in the more than fifty years I have known him, never said much to me beyond a singsong "Be a good boy, Lewie." Most of his working life was spent working on a laundry truck six days a week, ten hours a day, providing laundry service for people living in a poor and violent ghetto neighborhood in Newark, New Jersey. Although my father never put his message into words, on the basis of observing his behavior these many years and after much introspection, I have concluded that the following message is the central one he delivered to me about life:

"You know, Lew, I'm a frightened man. I'm just lucky no one has killed me yet. You know how hard my life is and how I never have any fun. I'm always suffering. Life is tough.

"You have to keep a smile on your face and be nice to people even if you hate them. Or they'll get you.

"My work is hard, but that's my destiny. Ever since I was a little boy I worked. At first I delivered newspapers and contributed to the family finances. I earned fifty cents a week and I usually gave my father the whole amount. One time I kept a penny for candy. When my father found out, he thrashed me. He believed we all had to contribute everything to the survival of our family.

"You need a woman. But they are really terrible people. They constantly nag you, and don't expect any sexual love from them. They don't really like sex. When they do it, it's only to get something out of you. When they do it, you should be grateful to them because they're doing you a favor. But they do cook, watch

31

the money and bring up the kids. You can't live with them and you can't live without them.

"Play the nice-guy role in life. Mask your anger. Never express it, or you'll get in trouble."

Knowing something about the powerful effects of a father's message, I have spent a considerable amount of time decoding his expressions to me and trying to live a life entirely different from his. For me, this resulted in a conscious decision, early in life, to not identify with my father's role in life in any way.

A son's identification with his father's role and his acceptance of his father's message depend on several factors: (1) whether the son has a genuine affection for his father; (2) whether the father is delivering his message to his son from a podium of profes-, sional, personal and emotional success; (3) whether his relationship to his father is intimate and emotionally intense; and (4) whether other important people in his life (notably his mother) encourage the boy to accept his father as a model. If all of these conditions prevail, a son is more apt to be accepting of his father's message, and his life will, therefore, be more deeply affected by his father.

COGNITIVE MAPS: DREAMS, HOPES AND REALITIES

A father's perception of the world is formed before his son's. Sons read the abstract or concrete bottom-line messages about life they get from their fathers. They have several possible responses. The two extremes are concordance and the decision to follow in their father's footsteps with him as a role model or, at the opposite end of the continuum, rebellion or rejection. The father's *cognitive map*, or his internal mental image of how his son could or should be, precedes the son's definition of his own life plan. The two perspectives can collide or be harmonious.

For my purposes here I define a cognitive map as the set of perceptions, hopes and dreams that a father has for his son, or, in reverse, the set of expectations a son has about his father.

Fathers usually have profound emotions related to career and other life choices made by their sons. Most caring fathers have dream maps about their sons' life choices—and most sons tend to have emotional reactions about their fathers' conceptions of their lives' directions.

On this issue, a father I interviewed, whose son had run away from home in the late sixties to join a commune, was in great anguish over his son's defection and rebellion. The father thought constantly about one statement his son had made to him: "Dad, why is it so important to you that I succeed in life on your terms?"

This is, of course, a key question all fathers and sons must ask themselves. Why does a father have or not have a clear concept of what his son will become in life? And why is this issue so important to most fathers? Some fathers obviously have a clear definition of what they want their sons to become; others care about their sons' goals but have an ill-defined concept of what they want their sons to become.

The effect of the father's cognitive map depends on the amount of closeness between the father and son, and how much they really love or care for each other. If a son cares a great deal about his father, it will affect what he does in response to his father's dream map for him. For example, in one interview I had with a son who cared a great deal for his father, he told me how he had overheard his father tell a friend in a casual conversation, almost in passing, that he would like his son to become a doctor. In this case the son, who was superconscious of his father's wishes, did attempt to become a doctor. On the other hand, sons who are hostile toward their fathers tend to rebel against anything their fathers want for them, and to go in the opposite direction.

Fathers who overlove or overcare for their sons often devote their lives to fulfilling every one of their sons' requests. Such fathers often sacrifice their own personal dreams for their sons, because of their intense level of caring. The degree of caring by a father, therefore, is a factor in determining the quality of the relationship, and the extent to which their respective dreams will be actualized.

Friction can occur between father and son when the son's life choices are not the same as those his father has made for him. A son may care a great deal about pursuing some occupational goal or marrying a particular woman. One or both of these choices may be unacceptable to the father. The level of caring for his father may thus produce a situation where the *valence*, or intensity, of his desire to pursue the occupation or marry the woman may supersede his level of caring for his father. Their dreams may collide into a dissonant situation of open conflict.

An interesting case in point involved a Jewish youth who presented his problem in a therapy group I ran. He fell in love with and wanted to marry out of his religion. His father was a rabbi who was dead set against his son's marriage to a gentile woman. The young man was deeply in love with his fiancée and would not be dissuaded by any argument. The father reminded his son that his health wasn't good. He had a heart condition, and he threatened his son with the possibility of a heart attack, should he marry the girl. The young man eloped and the father a few weeks later had a heart attack. Whether it was cause and effect or merely coincidence was impossible to determine. What became clear in the therapy group was that there was an enormous ambivalent role conflict in the son in his love for his wife and his love for his father. The son had to emotionally adjust his concern for his father to the demands of his father's dream plan for him to marry a Jewish girl. The son's defiance of his father's dream might have caused the father to have a heart attack. Both father and son had to adjust their cognitive maps in terms of their levels of caring.

Fortunately, the father recovered. During several counseling sessions with me on their problem, they were able to work out a solution, with both of them adjusting their positions. Basically the father loved his son, came to accept the fact that his son loved his wife and relinquished his expectations of his son marrying a Jew.

There are a number of films and literary works that depict this theme of dream dissonance. One that parallels the real life case of dissonance between the rabbi and his son is the film *The Jazz Singer*. In this fictional work, the father, a cantor, has a lifelong dream map that involves his son becoming a cantor like him and his father before him. The son's compulsion to succeed as a jazz singer supersedes his father's goals for him.

This theme of father-son dream conflict occurs in almost all cultures. A dramatic case in point is found in one segment of the film *Quartet*, based on one of Somerset Maugham's short stories about a British father and son. It is established early in the story that the father and son care a great deal about each other. The father is a very successful London businessman who wants his son to go into his business. The son wants to become a concert pianist.

The conflict between the father and son escalates as their dreams collide. Finally the father makes his son a proposition. He will finance his son's immediate dream for a year in Paris and provide him with the best music teachers available. There is one condition to the subsidy of his son's career. If at the end of the year the son does not have the talent to achieve his life's desire to become a concert pianist, as judged by a musical expert, he will put aside his goal and go to work in his father's business. The son agrees to the proposition because he cares enough about his father not to totally go against his wishes, and also he believes he has the talent to fulfill his dream.

At the end of the year he returns to the family home in London for the decision to be rendered on whose dream—the father's or the son's—will prevail. The son plays a recital for an elderly woman who is a highly respected concert pianist and acknowledged judge of talent. In the climactic scene the critic comes to their home, listens carefully with the rest of the family to his recital and renders her decision that the young man is talented, but clearly lacks the ability to become a first-rate concert pianist.

The son is emotionally demolished; the father is exuberant. In tears, the son goes upstairs to his room. As the family is saying goodbye to the judge, they hear a shot from upstairs. The young man has killed himself.

The young man, confronted with either giving up his life's dream or defying the father about whom he cares a great deal, chooses to end his life. Another dimension that one can speculate about was that, for the son, the suicide also served as an act of revenge, and was a form of punishment of the father.

Fathers and sons do not always communicate openly and honestly about their expectations of each other. Consequently, another vector in the mix of their dream maps and caring includes the *conscious* and *unconscious* motivations of fathers and sons.

The case of a delinquent teenager whom I met when I worked in a juvenile jail reflects the dynamics of unconscious motivations between a caring father and son. The son had been imprisoned because he had developed a pattern of running away from home which, of course, placed him in difficulty with the school and juvenile authorities. On the basis of approximately five intensive sessions I had with the young man, I pieced together the following picture of the dynamics that had developed between father and son.

The boy began running away from home shortly after the father, a long-distance truck driver, was grounded due to a back problem. The boy had a good school record up to the time his father was confined to the house. The pattern that emerged was that the boy would run away during the week and had begun to hitchhike pretty close to some of the routes his father used to take when he was on the road. The son would invariably return home on the weekend. His father would first briefly berate him for his transgressions. Then he would break out a six-pack of beer, and father and son would review every detail of the boy's week of adventure. The father would make comments like "Did you stop off at Annie's Café in Cincy? The chili there is sensational." In brief, the son had begun to live out his restricted father's unconscious desires, in a sense as a surrogate for his father, on the road.

An element that can compound the problem of dream dissonance between father and son occurs when there is limited *communication* between them, and they don't understand that their perceptions are different. This condition locks them into a conflict that can result in a lifelong serious problem.

When the father and son destroy, or seem to destroy, each other's dreams, it can lead to disappointment, disenchantment and conflict, especially when the father and son cannot communicate their dissatisfaction.

The father may punish the son for destroying his dream of what the son should be in his mind's eye. Beyond the physical or emotional punishment inflicted by some fathers, the son who is in his father's eyes the destroyer of his dream may even be killed. Death at the hands of the father can be the ultimate punishment for the destroyer of the dream.

A TV drama called *Richie,* based on a real-life incident, portrays this issue. The struggle revolves around Richie's drug addiction, a pathology that enormously disrupts the middle-class father's hopes for his son. Richie disappoints his father again and again by cleaning himself up and then returning to drugs. In a climactic fight scene, the son pulls a knife on his father and taunts his father to kill him, because he will never fulfill his father's dreams. The father inflicts the ultimate penalty on his son by shooting him to death in this, their final encounter. (The courts acquitted the real father about whom the TV drama was written.)

The following news report is another illustration of this dream destruction and death penalty punishment.

"A long-running feud between a father and son ended with a rifle shot and the death of 22-year-old Larry G.," authorities said.

"The father and his second eldest son had been at each other's throats for years, and this argument was the straw that broke it," the sheriff's sergeant said.

"The boy was out of work. He had lost a job. Before that he received a general discharge from the Marine Corps. The father was a hard-working man, a welder, and he couldn't understand his kid.

"Hot words led to hotter words. The old man told the kid to leave. He got his .22, the boy threatened him with a knife. The father pointed the gun. The boy lunged toward the father. The old man shot once, a reflex. He didn't know where he was aiming."[4]

The father killed his son. Further information on the case revealed the obvious. This hard-working middle-class father was enormously disappointed by the way his son had turned out.

Dream dissonance which leads to a father-son death penalty is found in many historical events. It was played out on a large and dramatic canvas in the life of Peter the Great of Russia. In piecing together this historic father-son drama, we find that Peter was a great man, but his dream dissonance with his son led to an abysmal tragedy. During the course of his distinguished career from the time he became the Czar of Russia at the age of ten in 1682, Peter helped to change the course of Russian history. He inherited a medieval country and converted it, during his reign, to a nation capable of playing an important role in international politics.

At six feet seven inches, Peter dwarfed men as his country dwarfed other nations. His passions were extreme and his energy seemingly unlimited. His son Alexis was a great disappointment to him, because the son had none of his father's energy and was of vastly different temperament. Peter treated his son with disdain and humiliated him on many occasions. In response to his father's shabby treatment, the son sought refuge abroad and may even have plotted against his father. In any case, Peter through his palace guard finally extracted a "confession" from his son that he had plotted to kill him, and he condemned his son to death. According to various historical reports, the boy died while being tortured before the execution.

In most cases of dream dissonance between father and son the struggle is restrained short of physical murder by the "little murders" of continuing arguments and fights. The conflicts are usually related to the fact that the fathers and sons merely have extremely different dreams about how the other should be.

One man I interviewed, now a psychologist in his sixties, never forgot the basic conflict he had with his father, a man who constantly picked on him because he (like Peter the Great's son) did not fit his father's desired image of a son. The psychologist grew up in Germany during the years when being or looking like a Jew was an undesirable situation.

"My father was basically dissatisfied with my size and looks. He constantly picked on me. He wanted more of a big Aryan son who reinforced his illusion of being non-Jewish. Actually he was half Jewish, and it was highly important in Germany at that time to not be Jewish at all. The real consequences were of course dangerous. I did not fit his idea of how his son should be [the father's cognitive map]. Nothing I did was good enough. He wanted me to be athletic but I was too short for most sports. I did get on the swimming team. My father only showed up at one meet which, incidentally, I won. My father's reaction was not to extol my virtues as a winner but to point out how terrible the other swimmers were. In this way he always discounted any of my achievements.

"Despite his many putdowns, my father was generous with material things. Perhaps he did that to compensate for the approval he never gave me in other areas of my life. He indulged me—let me drink, carouse, et cetera, as if to pay me off for what he would not give me emotionally. I never got his approval for the way I was.

"My father was consumed with a dream of being part of the upper classes. He married my mother because she was gentile and a countess. Because I was short and, in his eyes, Jewish-looking, he rejected me all his life. We never communicated about that subject. It's only now that I'm a psychologist that I can confront this issue. My most important dream in life was for his acceptance, something I never got."

A son can also have a dream for a father that is unfulfilled, and this can lead to disaster. One young man of twenty-five told me the following story of his relationship to his father.

"My father was and is a well-known and successful singer, but as a father he was and is a total flop. He abandoned my mother and me when I was ten. I had two images of fathers. One was very painful. I had a close friend who had a marvelous father. He was around, kind and sympathetic to all of my friend's needs. I always wished that man had been my father.

"My own father was a macho man. He always taught me never to cry or express my feelings. The few times I was with him he always had a lot of women around. Even on the rare occasions I would see him, he always had a broad—and I mean a broad—with him.

"My mother was obsessed with him and hated him. For the fifteen years after he left, I don't think a day went by that I didn't hear her say something vicious about him. After all those years of her propaganda, I shared her hatred toward him.

"So it wasn't a major surprise to me last year after I had been out drinking with him that I found myself standing over his drunk, passed-out body in bed in this New York hotel with his gun in my hand.

"I was slightly drunk myself. We'd been out with these bimbos and he had paid little attention to me. The whole night sitting there watching him play this nice guy, when I knew what a prick he had been to my mother and me, got me crazy.

"It was his gun that he always kept with him and I had it pointed at his head. My drunken reasoning was that I would blow him away for all the things he had never done for me as a father. Finally, luckily, I decided against killing him. Not because I didn't want to make up for all the things he never gave me as a father, but because I didn't want to destroy myself."

This was obviously an extreme reaction on the son's part, and there are other factors in his psychological makeup that led to his consideration of patricide. The basic problem, however, was that the disparity between his dream father and the real father was so great that it produced enormous hostility in him.

Sometimes the condition of dream dissonance is focused on a basic issue that can be resolved. The following case of a dream dissonance problem between father and son was focused on a particular area of conflict that was resolved in a therapy group attended by the father.

The father was a wealthy industrialist. He opened the session by bemoaning the fact that his only son, whom he dearly loved, rejected him and his ideas. "He never listens to my advice. It's so ridiculous—my employees, businessmen, all seek my advice and treasure it, but not my kid. He ignores me.'

"My son doesn't love me. I can't even talk to him. The only way I can talk to him is if he is in his room with the door locked. I stand outside the door like a schmuck and talk to him through the door. It's absolutely humiliating. That's the only time he will answer me. I don't understand all of this. I've given him everything I have. He will own the whole business one day. I told him it's his. I don't deserve this kind of treament from him. I feel awful."

The father's hidden agenda, his dream for his son, emerged in a later group session. The father was obsessed with his business. It was his creation and treasure. He had worked hard to make this business successful, and he saw it as a shrine to be passed on to his only son who would then become the keeper of the flame. His dream was that his son would take over his business and he, the father, would then live in the reflected glory of his son. The son would become his *creation*, his *ego extension*. The son smashed the father's dream by rejecting any role in his father's business. The father perceived this as a personal rejection of him and his achievements in life. In effect it was, since the son had evolved another plan for his life.

The father obfuscated his own needs to have his son confirm the validity of his hard work by playing the role of an unselfish, martyred father. "I worked so hard for one reason—to have my son have a better life. I wanted to give my son a chance to really enjoy the luxuries and affluence I have created." In reality, he wanted his son to carry on in his reflected glory for his own emotional aggrandizement.

In one session I posed the key question that had to be answered by the father: "Can you get rid of your dream fixation to have your son go into your business without losing your love for your son? In other words, can you still love your son if he does not fullfill your dream?" The group further pointed out to the father that his love for his son was contingent on the son's acquiescence to the father's need to control him and to the father's plan that he live out the aspiration the father had for the two of them. As the man began to examine this basic question, he began to cry. My analysis was that he was crying about giving up his fixated dream for his son and himself. His tears were tears of grief for a dream he had for his son, a dream that had to die if they were going to relate to each other. The father's therapeutic sessions and his crying allowed him to verbalize and to communicate the cognitive dream fixation that he had to give up. And he further had to confront the fact of loving his son without the necessity of his son's capitulation to his personal dream.

In a group psychodrama he was told to dictate a letter that he was to later actually write to his son, who was at the time away at college. The father soliloquized:

"Dear Son:

"I have been dismayed by the lack of communication between us and have tended to blame you for it. I now see that you are avoiding me for a reason. I have examined the nature of my complications and conflict with you in therapy. I remember as long as we talked about music and sports, we could talk. At least we could listen to each other. [Analysis: neither father nor son wanted to hear the other's dream because it intruded on each of their autonomous hopes in a fundamental way. They avoided confrontation on this highly emotional issue of conflict.]

"As you know, I have gone into therapy because of my pain about our relationship. I figured out in my therapy that you wanted to go into theater arts, in part because anything removed from my interests or control was what you wanted. I now realize you are a separate person with your own life dreams. I now admit I was controlling, manipulative and wrong.

"I will never bring up again the professional direction you are taking or my former hopes that you would enter my business. I can see now I was wrong and I want you to forgive me. I was concerned with getting my own personal success through you. [Analysis: the father concluded his son was into his own dreams of success and he had to bite the bullet and surgically exorcise his son from his personal dream.]

"I am voluntarily cutting you loose from my expectations of you without inducing guilt in you and without any punitive action. You will share in the profits of my business and I have gladly written my will so you will inherit my resources, along with Mom, on my demise.

Love,
Dad"

The son called his father after he received the letter. He thanked his father for understanding how he really felt. The next time the two met, their ability to communicate was greatly improved.

A father or son who gives up his emotional plan of how the other can fulfill his dreams has to reorganize his priorities in life, and this can be a painful process. However, this process can result in an enormous emotional plus for the father, in the form of stress reduction. In the case of this father, giving up his dreams for his son enabled him to relax and stop feeling the constant strain of pushing the son to do something he did not want to do. When the father gave up his dream it eliminated the tension in their relationship. They began to communicate effectively and became good friends.

Fathers and sons can adjust their dreams to fit their loved ones' feelings when they become aware of the dream dissonance factor. Most emotionally healthy people can accept feedback information and tear up or revise their cognitive dream maps when they are out of touch with the desires of their loved ones. When a father and son understand their dream dissonance they can revise their hopes more in accord with reality. Effective communication with each other about the situation can produce the necessary awareness to resolve the conflict and provide emotional relief for both parties.

Lacking in a pathological father-son relationship is the ability to communicate, confront, *work through* and adjust to their conflicts and the concomitant frustrations that constitute their situation. A lack of real communication often leads to a false accommodation between father and son. Under such conditions each has a hidden agenda of constant anger toward the other that impedes solution and ultimately leads to emotional exhaustion and, in many cases, the desire to punish each other.

In my own therapeutic practice I have observed many sons trying to please their fathers by *accommodation*. This leads to a robotlike unfeeling personality. The son who castrates himself and denies his dreams in order to please his father can develop a severe neurosis that involves lifelong emotional pain for both father and son. The son can become emotionally dead in this accommodation process, since he subverts his need to confront his real emotions, and the father can cast himself into an uncomfortably despotic role over his son. This leads to a painful lifelong struggle between a father and son.

I recall a psychodrama session where a son who had accommodated his own self to his father's wishes all his life was full of fury and hostility. In the session he presented a scene in a hospital where he attempted to express his real feelings before his father died of cancer. According to the son, the session was an accurate scenario of the scene that had actually taken place at the father's deathbed. (A member of the group was cast in the role of his father.)

SON: Dad, I have something to tell you.
L.Y.: Hold it. Before you pour your feelings out to your dying father, soliloquize what you are thinking and prepare your speech.
SON (*to group*): I want to tell my father about all the misery he caused me in my life by forcing me to live my life by his standards. I became a lawyer for his sake, not mine. I wanted to do something else. All my life I accommodated myself to his ego demands and needs. Here at his deathbed I wanted to tell him how I really felt about his controlling me all my life and how I still loved him in spite of the fact that he was a dictator. Finally I was going to show him that I was a bigger man than he, because I was also going to forgive him.
L.Y.: Okay. Go ahead and tell your father about all of these feelings you have kept inside you all these years.
SON: Dad, I know you're near the end and I want to tell you something.
FATHER: Before you do, son, I want to tell *you* something. I forgive you for all your bad behavior.
SON (*to group*): That's exactly what he said. Before I could tell him what I wanted to say and then forgive him, he died right then and there, and left me totally frustrated.

In the psychodrama session we gave the son an opportunity to pour out his lifelong list of grievances to his "father" (someone in the role of an auxiliary who played his father). During the session, he also explored the reasons why he had accommodated his father's needs over his own. He punched a pillow held by the person playing his father as he recited his long list of grievances. After he had exhausted his anger and frustration through this device, he could feel the underlying love he had for his father, which he expressed by hugging the auxiliary-ego father and finally forgiving him. He acknowledged feeling much better after the session. He felt that the psychodrama, although not as satisfying as telling his real father before he died, had been adequate for relieving many of the negative feelings he was carrying around inside himself. He further felt that understanding the fact of the dream dissonance conflict between him and his father was a valuable insight.

The basic problem of dream dissonance between fathers and sons is often subtle and hidden. It also may be intermittent; that is, it may only appear at certain times in the relationship. Because fathers are older and, hopefully, wiser, greater knowledge and understanding about their dreams and messages in their father role can help alleviate many of the problems and conflicts that emerge between fathers and sons.

CHAPTER TWO
Father Styles

ALL MEN ARE sons, but not all men become fathers. Some men are frightened by the responsibilities of becoming a father, and assume the role very irresponsibly, with little or no concern about its meaning and impact on their son's personality.

An important intangible variable in defining a father's style with his son is the desire and passion with which a father embraces the role. Personal freedom of choice has increasingly become a factor, especially with the advent of effective contraceptive devices, including vasectomy and the liberation of many men from sociocultural and religious imperatives toward fatherhood.

Since the decision of whether to become parents has been placed more firmly in the hands of both men and women, having a child is a more voluntary activity. Control over the possibility of fatherhood means that men usually assume this role because they find it desirable. There are probably fewer disgruntled parents today as compared to previous times, when there was less control over the eventuality of parenthood.

Many men refuse to assume the role out of fear, for selfish reasons, or as a way of asserting their social protest against the problems of overpopulation. Men who choose *not* to become fathers do so after considerable thought, for personal reasons. As one man bluntly told me: "I don't want to contaminate my life work with the need to support and raise children." He may be excluding a certain amount of joy from his life, but being childless will unquestionably eliminate many demanding annoyances and responsibilities, and give him more time to live his life his way. Becoming a father should not be an automatic response by men in our overpopulated and increasingly complex world.

There is substantial evidence that most fathers are emotionally involved with their children from conception through birth. Impending fatherhood in the old "B" movies portrayed a heroic man full of joy at his wife's cryptic announcement. In reality, many men experience a variety of acute anxieties as a result of memories of their own unhappy childhood, of rivalry with brothers and sisters, a fear of competition with the new child for the wife's affection or the closing off of escape from an unhappy marriage. Research indicates that these insecure men approaching fatherhood feel severe depression, loss of appetite, insomnia or delusions of illness.

A veteran obstetrician divided men into three general classes in their reactions to and behavior during their wives' pregnancies: (1) the father who shows a reasonable amount of concern and understanding toward his pregnant wife and participates in the prenatal program; (2) the macho father-to-be who has the instincts and sensibilities of a bull, and believes he has done his duty by inseminating his female and that the consequences are her problem, not his. He has a minimal interest in the progress of his wife's pregnancy and is resentful when it interferes with the regular routine of her household duties as it affects his personal comforts; and (3) the "pregnant" father who overidentifies with his wife. He is just the opposite of the macho man. He worries excessively, tries to interpret the meaning of every new physical symptom, reads about every new "system" of childbirth.

Being a father is one of the few irrevocable commitments a man can make in life. He can divorce his wife or leave his parents, but remaining with and caring for his child, sometimes because of binding cultural and religious imperatives, keep him committed in a deep emotional way.

Part of the fear of fathering is related to the fact that a man has to carry out his role in a complex society which affords him little or no training. It is within this amorphous nondirective framework that fathers assume the *life sentence* of being a father. It is no wonder that many men plagued with their own personal inadequacies, the fear of reliving their own abominable childhood through their child and lack of success in the world at large, flee from the role, or try to distance themselves from its obligations.

A man's father style is determined by the dynamic interplay of some or all of the following forces: his enthusiasm for the role; his own father as a role model; the images of how to be a father projected by the mass media; the man's occupational role; the social, legal, cultural, economic, class and religious orientation of the man; the man's unique personality, character and temperament (e.g., is he "hyper" or calm, a stressed or nonstressed person, methodical or flighty?); the unique and specific sociometric structure and familial problems of orientation and procreation at different points in time; and the number of other children already in the family. (On this last point, a comic on a talk show commented that he had four children. He said, "The first one was the practice throwaway kid." It is apparent that later children grow up in a different family from that of the first child.)

One of the most significant influences on a father's style with his son is the imprint of his own father's style as a model for him. It is consciously and unconsciously a factor that is always at work. Many men discipline their sons, counsel them and "love" them like their own father did.

The "training" a son receives to become a father by observing and emulating his father as a role model can often be disastrous when the father provides a negative image. There is ample evidence that the sons of child-batterers, criminals and addicts repeat the sins of their fathers with their own children. In so-called "criminogenic families," there is a social inheritance of criminality which is passed on from one generation to the next, and this is often the result of the continuance of negative fathering.

In some cases where there is a negative role model, a son's rebellion produces an individual who is enormously different from his father. In one interview the respondent commented: "My father was so terrible with me that I consciously worked to undo his harm. He was cold and distant and I knew the pain of being his son. With my own boy I went to the opposite extreme. My father never hugged me once—I always hug my son and stay close to him."

The sociohistorical context is important in understanding a father's style. In one interview, a fifty-year-old man described how his "loving father" beat him unmercifully when he came home late from school. Without the description of the context and the time period, it would appear that the father's discipline practice was overkill. Yet when the man explained the context of the father-son interaction during the time his father beat him, it was apparent that the beatings had another meaning. The man grew up in Rome during World War II when it was dangerous to be on the streets, and in this context his father's disciplinary approach made sense. The man was a loving father intent on saving his son's life. The father's harsh disciplinary style was of limited use to his son in his American cultural setting.

The mass media reflect and have some impact on men's fathering styles. However, they are a highly debatable source of fathering education, since most of the father images projected on TV and in feature films are apt to reflect a commercial writer's fantasy. Most of the images of fathers that appear on TV or movie screens are absurd, and bear a limited relationship to reality. Is there a father anywhere who can emulate the perspicacity, patience and prudence of Ozzie Nelson, or Robert Young as the father in *Father Knows Best?* Or how many loving fathers are there who replicate the wonderfully kind white millionaire who adopts two black children in the TV comedy *Different Strokes?* Despite the many false flickering images depicted in the mass media, there are many accurate and insightful cinematic portraitures of fathers and sons. These include films like *Ordinary People* and *Kramer vs. Kramer.*

Among the films that produce insights into the father-son relationship is *The Great Santini.* The film, based on the book of the same name by Pat Conroy, depicts the real-life struggles of the author with his father. It fundamentally reveals how the father's occupational role as a Marine Corps fighter pilot is transferred to his fathering style. As such, it accurately and dramatically presents the dynamics in the relationships of many real-life fathers and sons I have researched.

Because of his military orientation, Bull Meechum is a remote father, except when he comes home on leave. The long periods of separation of the son from his father place the father in a heroic, distant position vis-à-vis the son and the rest of the family. The son can fantasize positive, brave, courageous images of his father in his mind's eye, because he seldom sees his father. These heroic images of the father are reinforced by the mother, who in this case was a positive transmitter of the father's image.

The film begins with the father's return to the States after a tour of European duty. We see how happy the family is to have him back. We see the father's style as an authoritarian "by-the-numbers" controlling figure with his family. He is a man who, as an officer, asserts his control in a military fashion over other people, and this occupational aspect of his life is carried over into his father-style control of his family, including his son.

The father sees his occupation as a combat Marine officer in peacetime as flawed by a major deficiency. The ingredient missing in his life is a war. And he recites General Patton-type lines about how difficult it is for a warrior to function without a war.

The father, in keeping with his military macho demeanor, perceives the world as full of enemies. He attempts to convince his son that toughness is the basic, if not the only, masculine trait that is to be nurtured. He turns on his wife one night and accuses her of trying to make her son soft. Softness to him is akin to death. There is an element of validity in his tough perception of the world, since in the military, a man can literally be killed if he's not tough or lets down his guard.

In one key scene in the film, at a high school championship basketball game, we see the son, a star basketball player, knocked down by another player during the game. The bellicose father, who is patrolling the stands, loudly orders his son to take revenge, and threatens to refuse to let him into his home if he doesn't do so. The son promptly and brutally knocks down his adversary and breaks his arm. Later, the son deeply regrets following his father's harsh order. The incident reveals how the son, a fundamentally kind person, is torn between his basic emotions and his desire to please his macho father. For the father, brutality and paranoia go with his territory, but it is a posture that the son rejects. These issues form the basic conflict between father and son. The son has great difficulty fulfilling the requirements that his father's style demands.

In a climactic scene, in the middle of the night, the son hears the sounds of his father beating his mother. He enters the fray and defends his mother by knocking his father down. This leads to a period of estrangement between the father and son. The father later dies in a military plane crash. Guilt-ridden and in tears, the son confesses to his grieving mother that he prayed for his father's death so he could be free. The mother tells him that he became free from his macho father's tyranny and control the night he defended her and stood up to him. The basic theme of the story reveals how the son, who loved his father, comes to understand why his father behaved as he did, and his final rejection of his father's macho style for a more compassionate role in life.

As indicated in *The Great Santini*, a father's occupational role is a significant factor in its effect on his father style. It not only affects a son's image of the father style he might adopt, but it can have very real effects on the social, emotional and financial legacy he receives from his father.

In today's highly complex technological society with its extreme diversity of occupations, the odds are low that a son will follow his father as a role model in his choice of occupation. The father and son thus miss out on a significant bonding factor that they could benefit from. Sons who do enter their fathers' professions probably spend more time with them. Such fathers and sons also usually go through life with an added dimension of communication and a closer understanding of each other's needs, problems and victories.

The effect of working for my father on a part-time basis on his laundry truck was to convince me that any other line of work was better than his. However, the experience was a very valuable one for me in learning more about how and why my father's occupation affected his father sytle.

I would periodically go out on the road with my father on his laundry truck, picking up and delivering laundry. His route happened to be in the poorest, most violent ghetto in Newark, New Jersey. Working with my dad was, for me, the most valuable, affectionate and communicative aspect of our father-son relationship. (I believe my contact through my father with this milieu of poverty inspired me to become a sociologist.)

While working on the truck together, my father and I would discuss his business, its trials and rewards. I knew how hard my father worked because I saw him in action. I quickly concluded, based on my experiences on the road, that his was an occupation that I did not want to pursue. In fact, I was motivated to find an occupation as remote from my father's as possible.

One factor that sharpened my resistance to following in his occupational footsteps was the abject depression he experienced when his truck was stolen and remained missing for over a week. The police never recovered the truck. I did. I went out on my bicycle all through the neighborhood and I finally found it, abandoned on a vacant lot with all the bundles gone.

My father was almost paralyzed with emotional depression when the truck was stolen. After I recovered the truck he was in tears, because he couldn't find a way to tell his customers about their clothing, which had been stolen from the truck. In a crisis, my mother would come through for my father, and she gave him the courage to start over. He went from customer to customer, assessing what he owed them. Some lied, others were compassionate and told my father to forget it and resume laundry service.

In brief, I went through this life trauma with my father and was able to help him survive. Our relationship at that time was interlocking. I knew and felt his pain, and then his relief when the situation had been resolved. What became clear to me then, as an adolescent, was that I *never* wanted to experience what he did. I accurately associated his pain with his difficult occupation. Here was a man who ground out a rather meager living (between thirty-five and fifty dollars a week for a family of five), worked about ten hours a day, six days a week, and could almost be destroyed by one traumatic event such as the robbery. His occupational status affected his father style because his position rendered him a joyless person. His work was drudgery and it made him a drudge as a father and a man. His despondency when he temporarily lost his business left me with a lasting fear. To this day, although I rationally know it couldn't happen, I have a fear that one mishap could leave me without a profession. In brief, I saw my father as a negative role model, largely because of his difficult occupation.

Low-status occupations have their effect on a father's style. However, men in high-status occupations also have their problems. High socioeconomic status in our patrilineal society sets up complex issues of status, maintenance, legacies and the inheritance of wealth and status by sons. High-status fathers in important jobs almost automatically have a patriarchal autocratic father style because there is wealth and position to be maintained, and ultimately handed down to the son. The sons of such fathers are usually in line for some legacy, in contrast to sons who have poor, powerless fathers.

Sometimes the legacy of a high-status, and particularly that of a celebrity, father is a mixed blessing. In addition to his father's famous name, his financial position and the possible inheritance of some talent, a son can also inherit the legacy of an unreasonable expectation of success that he cannot possibly fulfill.

Moreover, the style of a high-status or celebrity father will almost inevitably be influenced by a variety of corrupting factors. There is a disparity in most celebrity fathers between the public image and the real self. The demands of continued success are enormous in terms of personal energy and time. Highly visible celebrity fathers are besieged by their public, and this can severely reduce the amount of time such fathers can spend with their children, and the places in which they can spend that time.

As the son of a celebrity told me, "Everybody wants a piece of him. When I was a kid, even if he had the time—which he didn't —we could never go to Disneyland, the movies or anywhere in public together. The few times we did, he was mobbed and I was pushed aside."

In brief, the demands of the celebrity role in society have a profound effect on a man's father style. Because of the requirements of his lifestyle he usually has a limited amount of quality time for his children. His children have to separate their father from his public image. His son may have some advantages because of the family name and status of his father; however, the son's achievements in life will invariably be compared to his father's successes, especially if he enters his father's occupation.

One twenty-one-year-old son of a celebrity father, a well-known TV personality, reflected the common experience of other sons of celebrity fathers I interviewed:

"When I was a kid in grade school I knew my father was

special because of the way my teachers fawned on me. In high school it wasn't just the teachers, it was also my friends. I never knew who my real friends were because I found out that a lot of them wanted to come over to my house just to see my father. The only guys I felt comfortable with were kids whose fathers were as well known as Dad was.

"What was the message my father gave me? He said very little to me because he wasn't around much. I saw him more on TV than in person. Even though he never said anything, I always felt I had to be a big success in life. His unspoken message was 'Be a success, but you'll never make it as big as I have!'

"I've always carried that burden around with me. And as you know, I've done a lot of drugs, and fucked up in different ways. As a result of a lot of therapy I concluded that I don't have to be a big success. Learning that simple fact has reduced the pressure I always felt from my dad.

"Now I'm much more relaxed. I never want to go into show business, because I would automatically be compared to my dad. When I graduate from college, I'm going to law school, and I'll strike out on my own."

This young man averted many of the problems sons of celebrities face by going into a different field from his father's, and rejecting the implicit message that he had to be a success.

A special problem the sons of celebrity fathers face is that society confers on such young men a certain amount of prestige, and rewards that they have not earned. There are many people who will pay special attention to a Franklin Roosevelt, Jr., a John Barrymore, Jr., or a Winston Churchill, Jr., simply because of who his father has been—rather than what *he* does. This instant positive response can cause the son to feel empty, nondeserving, and sometimes guilty because he feels the special attention he receives is unearned by him. He never knows if he is receiving personal or professional acceptance from others because of his unique personality or ability, or because he is the son of a celebrity.

Kathy Cronkite discussed the problems of children of celebrity fathers in her book *On the Edge of the Spotlight*. In this book, based on her own life and interviews with twenty-six children of famous parents, she came to a number of conclusions about the positive and negative impacts of having a celebrity father. Ms. Cronkite writes about how she spent much of her life on the edge of the spotlight. Family meals in restaurants were often interrupted when fans approached the table to ask her father for his autograph. And when people did talk to Kathy, the first words out of their mouths often were to ask her what it was like to be Walter Cronkite's daughter.

In her book she commented: "I can remember once having an intimate conversation with my father and a man came up to us and pushed me aside and asked him what he thought about the Middle East. I was actually pushed and shoved out of the way by this man. When you're thirty, you can deal with it, but when you're six or sixteen, it's hard to take."[1]

The book was written in memory of Paul Newman's son, Scott Newman, who died in 1978 of a self-inflicted drug overdose. He and Kathy became friends after she moved to Hollywood to start her acting career. Regarding an experience she had at a party with Scott, she commented:

"One evening I heard Scott drunkenly accuse someone of being interested in him only because of his father, when in fact the 'antagonist' did not even know who his father was. Later at the same party he said belligerently to someone else, 'Don't you know who my father is?' "[2]

Scott Newman's tragedy was a partial result of his also being on the edge of the spotlight. He worked sporadically as a stunt man in the movies. I acquired an in-depth interview with one of his sisters, who felt a deep involvement with her brother's problems as the son of a celebrity father. She felt she had many of the same problems experienced by her brother. Her comments about the relationship between Scott and Paul Newman are of value in understanding the general problems that a celebrity father automatically acquires, and how this can affect his son's life.

"One night we were all having dinner in our home in Brentwood. Dad and Mom were there and two of my sisters. After dinner I went to the back of the house to wash some clothes and I saw this face with glasses behind the locked gate. At first it

55

scared me—then I saw who it was. It was Scott. It was kind of eerie to see him behind this big iron gate, because it reminded me of how he had put himself out there, really outside our family, looking in. It was about a year before he died of an overdose of 'ludes and alcohol.

"I remember we talked for a long time that night sitting out by the back door. The thing I remember most about our conversation was that one minute he was saying how much he loved me, Dad and the family, and how bad he felt about the way things were, and how he couldn't seem to get it together. The next minute his face would get cold and angry and he would become insulting and almost violent. That night as we talked he became hostile and got pretty loud. My father must have heard him because around that time my dad came to the back door and said, 'What's going on out there?' Dad really wanted to talk to him. I know Dad loved him a lot and really wanted to help, but somehow it didn't work. At that time Scott said that he didn't want to talk to him. I remember Scott told me that all the talking he had done with Dad and to shrinks had done him no good.

"Dad did his best. I remember when I was younger they would go a lot of places together. And Dad would talk to him a lot. But, of course, Dad was always superbusy. And when he was making a movie he just wasn't available. I'm sure Scott wanted a lot more time with him than he got.

"When someone you love and need can only see you now and then for just a few hours, you feel love and hate. When you really love someone as Scott loved Dad, you hate the fact that he can't be with you. I think that's the reason Scott had a lot of anger in him.

"There are many good things about being in our family. One thing is that you know there is always a hand or a safety net to catch you if you fall. There's always money, and then there's the name. You always go to the limit of anything you do, because you think how far that name can take you. Scott maybe figured he would be rescued at the last minute. But the hand didn't appear.

"All my life—and I'm sure this was true of Scott too—I felt I had to be famous and successful. It's only recently that I figured out, 'Hey, you really don't have to be famous if you don't want to.' Figuring that out has relaxed me and made me feel happier. Maybe Scott never figured that out. And he died trying to be another Paul Newman. He could never succeed because my dad is one of a kind."

Scott Newman lived in the shadow of his father's public image, and no doubt this always affected their relationship. Paul Newman's comment on the personal situation created by his public image is of value in understanding the role of other fathers who are celebrities. "Some of my relatives and people close to me are able to use my name and benefit from it. Others, like my son, might have been hurt by my public image. In the final analysis, even if I could, I can't change who I am for the people I love. I want my loved ones to prosper but I can't always help them the way they want me to. I have to live my own life the best way I know how and I can't change who I am."

The comment is appropriate for men from all positions in society. Fathers who are celebrities, however, are apt to have their father styles affected by their public images and successes. Few men can remain totally unaffected by great success and public acclaim. A tendency toward egocentrism is bound to creep into their personalities, and all these factors are bound to affect their father styles.

In the same way that a man's status can profoundly affect his father style, his cultural, ethnic or religious background can do so as well. There appear to be significant differences in the ways men from American, Irish, Italian or Jewish backgrounds develop their father styles in the context of their family structures.

A study by Doctors Paul Barrabee and Otto Von Mering of Harvard University, "Ethnic Variations in Mental Stress," provides considerable data on prototypical father styles in different sociocultural ethnic-religious milieus. The authors studied sixty-nine American families of Irish, Italian, Jewish and Yankee origins.[3]

They found that the typical Irish father remains somewhat detached from his son but maintains a supervisory right that is all-inclusive. Like the mother, the father frequently belittles his son about his appearance and behavior to make him feel subordinate, which is very stressful for the son and resented by him.

However, the Irish son does not seem to develop strongly negative emotional reactions toward his father. According to the study, the son is apt to accept his subordination to his father with little conflict, because the number of situations in which he experiences subordination is small in comparison to the amount he experiences with his mother.

The research implied that the Irish-American mother has the main disciplinary responsibility even though the father remains the head of the household. One forty-year-old man I interviewed who came from this type of Irish-American background described his father's style and the disciplinary situation in his family as follows:

"My father was a working man, not educated, wise in his own way, a man full of laughter and good feelings. He was a big man and very strong, but I never saw him deliberately hurt anyone or anything. He never laid a hand on my brother or me. I suppose the thing I feared most, oddly enough, was the rather desperate rage he seemed to display whenever one of us was injured.

"I recall once cutting my brow open while playing football, and running home with the blood streaming into my eye, less concerned about the injury than about the fact that my father would grow angry (what seemed like anger—passed for anger—to a boy) when he was confronted with it. I've since concluded that he was not angry at us. He wanted to protect my brother and me from any kind of hurt. Perhaps not the wisest thing, but certainly very loving.

"When I was twenty I began to suffer from abdominal pain and night sickness that defied, for a while, any attempts at diagnosis, until the bad appendix finally revealed itself. That night the pain and distress were so great that I left my bed and went into the living room. My father, sensitive to any stirrings in the house, got up and came in to see what was the matter. There was nothing much to be done at that lonely hour of the night. The idea of calling emergency never occurred to either of us, since our well-respected physician had assured us that the surgery scheduled for the following week was quite soon enough. And so my father sat with me and, in fact, tried to cuddle me, and take some of my pain in that mystical, unreasoning way, although I found it somehow embarrassing to be treated so like a child. Yet I was comforted by it.

"When we were young, discipline came directly and immediately from my mother, who had the care of us most of the time as was commonplace in that era. Rarely did she use the threat of telling our father of our misbehavior when he came home from work, which would have deferred the need to punish and relegated that unhappy duty to the male. But that's not to suggest for a moment that he was not the head of the household, if that title is defined as one who has the principal financial responsibility and is looked to as the ultimate protector of the family members. How did he establish discipline with his sons? I don't know what my brother would say, but I often asked myself, before venturing to do something out of the commonplace, whether my father would be hurt or shamed by it if it became public.

"There is another gentle deception which we all played. If my brother and I insisted on acting up at bedtime, and if we ignored repeated warnings, my mother would threaten that my father would come in and whack us with the long-handled brush used to clean behind the radiators. My father would come charging into our bedroom with the brush and whack the bedclothes at our feet unmercifully, never striking us even a glancing blow, while my brother and I scrunched under the covers and laughed. We were, my father, brother and I, conspirators in a plot against my mother's authority over us. But actually I'm certain we knew then, as we were able to express with certainty later on, that my mother was in on the deception all the time.

"Whatever it was, it worked."

Jewish families tend to produce a unique father-mother-son configuration. The Harvard researchers found in Jewish families a configuration that supports my own research findings. The Jewish mother is apt to be overprotective and overtly affectionate. She employs guilt-producing techniques and the withdrawal of love as her primary means of control.

The typical Jewish father is not very punishing, but, like his son, yields much of the control over his life to his wife. The Jewish son, therefore, is not likely to have strong negative feelings toward his father because the father in this constellation has limited power. However, because his father tends to be a pathetic, powerless figure, the son is less likely to accept his father as a role model, as is the case in other family configurations.

My own Jewish family situation supports the findings of the Harvard family research. My father was dominated by my repressive and chastising mother. Because of this family structure, my own father's disciplinary style was typical of many Jewish fathers whom I interviewed. My mother was the basic disciplinarian and my father, at times, after much chastisement by her, would take me aside for discipline. In effect he asserted very little of his own authority as a father.

The pattern of his discipline was uniform when I was a teenager. He would say, "Why are you aggravating your mother? You know how nervous she is. Do you want her to go nuts like your Aunt Minnie? For God's sake, behave yourself." He would follow up this guilt-inducing method that shifted the emphasis from my bad behavior to my mother's problems by citing the great rationalizer—"She's going through her changes [menopause]."

His discipline conveyed several points: he had no point of view about my bad behavior; the only thing wrong with what I did was that it aggravated my mother and she would then turn her hostility on him; also, I might drive her off the emotional edge. ("She's going through her changes.") The process also allied us against her. ("Don't 'bring heat' or exasperate her—keep the peace.") He, like most *nebbish* Jewish fathers with a strong "Yiddishe momma" wife, never acted on his own. He was mainly her agent in the process, and was attempting self-defense from her smoldering wrath that might burst into flame at a moment's notice.

For most of my life I was hostile toward my tyrannical mother. It was at a rather late date (when I was around forty) that I concluded that my "Yiddishe poppa" and his frightened, nonassertive father style were more of a problem than my mother and her overt attitude. I felt that if he had stood up to her and controlled her more, it would have been a healthier emotional situation for all of us. My father, Harry, because of his own Jewish cultural roots (a reflection of his father and mother), presented a typically Jewish weak-father style.

In the Barrabee and Von Mering study, it was found that the Italian son was the recipient of sex-linked preferential treatment from both his parents. There was little concern with affection and practically no overt display of it. The Italian mother was likely to be oversolicitous, partly due to the superior status of males and partly due to her concern over her son's physical welfare. The father's rigidity and propensity for administering physical punishment induced the mother to act as a buffer between father and son. The son reacted to this situation by feeling obligated to carry out maternal commands without hesitation, which increased his emotional dependence on the mother. While the son enjoyed the protection provided by his mother against his father, neither parent showed interest in his personal problems. Moreover, the father's extreme strictness tended to create a fear-ridden respect for him in the son. The son felt unable to reject the father as a role model.

In the Harvard study, the typical American Yankee father was not very dominant, nor was he inclined to make much use of physical punishment. He was likely to be rejected as a role model, but also was not apt to be the object of the intense feelings the son felt toward his mother. The great difficulties in identifying with his father in a specific area of conduct and in having to rely almost exclusively on his mother's emotional guidance appear to be very stressful to the study's Yankee son. The Yankee mother uses the withdrawal-of-love technique to control more widely than any other, but she differs from the Jewish mother in her emphasis on the moral and religious implications of transgression rather than its impact upon her personal feelings. The vague pervasiveness of the moral implications of all his conduct appears to be highly stressful to the typical Yankee son, who responds to his mother with a deep emotionality that contains a high degree of guilt and a strong sense of inadequacy. The prototype of the Yankee father began with the strong patriarchal image of the rural father who emulated or paralleled our country's founding fathers. They were characterized as supermen who took care of their family's physical and emotional needs and at the same time forged a civilization out of the wilderness.

They were tough but loving fathers. Lorne Greene's fictional portrait in *Bonanza* of the "King of the Ponderosa" was that of a patriarch who fulfilled the ideals of the rural father. Another positive stereotype imbedded in the American psyche by the mass media was Judge Hardy (Lewis Stone), the father of Andy Hardy (Mickey Rooney). In the thirties and forties the Andy Hardy movies were seen by vast audiences. People felt secure in viewing the typical American relationship of Judge Hardy and his "dingaling" son Andy.

Pure American sons in those days never fooled with drugs or "went all the way" with a girl. In those days of no pills or sophisticated contraceptives, a kiss was the apparent end point between teenagers. Usually, however, about three-quarters of the way into the typical Andy Hardy movie, Andy was in trouble. The "trouble" by today's standards was minuscule. Nevertheless, the matter was invariably resolved when Mom referred Andy to his omniscient, wise old dad who, in his classic-Americana man-to-man talks, would solve his son's problem. Of course, the problems were simple ones. They never involved modern-day teenage problems like getting the clap, being strung out on heroin, knocking up the starry-eyed girlfriend or being busted for armed robbery. These earlier American perceptions and images of an Andy Hardy-type son and Judge Hardy-type father still prevail in small rural middle-American areas. But these elements comprise an American father-son style that is rapidly disappearing from the cultural landscape as these smaller communities become urbanized and confront big-city social problems.

BASIC TYPES OF FATHER STYLES

As a result of the impact of various socioeconomic and cultural factors, the imprint of his own father as a role model, his unique personality and other social influences, a man develops his unique father style. My research showed some central elements of father styles which seemed to be the core way a father acts out his role in his dynamic relationship to his family. Most fathers, including both loving and cold, distant ones, go through periods of a love-hate relationship with their sons, even though the basic style of relating to their sons remains constant. A basically compassionate father can be competitive at some phase of his relationship to his son. Almost all fathers do, however, develop some basic modality of a father style. The following styles emerge as basic types adopted alone or in some combination by American fathers.

1. *Compassionate Loving-Doubling Fathers* A father of this type is generally an emotionally healthy man. He is capable, when it is appropriate, of placing his son's needs ahead of his own. He is able to give of himself and place his son in a central role in his life. His son's needs usually take precedence over his own needs, and this reveals the intensity of his compassion and love for his son.

He is capable of doubling with his son. By doubling, I mean the ability of a father to become *one* with his son's emotions rather intensely in his early years, and to place himself inside his son's self when necessary in his later years. Doubling enables him to feel his son's joy and pain. It is a form of loving that requires an intense kind of empathy—the ability to accurately take the role of his son in significant emotional situations.

This father type usually wanted a son in his life plan. He borders on being poetic and lyrical about the birth of his son. He perceives the birth of his son almost as the fulfillment of, or at least as one of the epochal experiences in, his own life. The following verbatim comments by a man of fifty recalling his early years with his son capture his doubling quality:

"The night he was born—a beautiful fall evening in a small hospital by the Mediterranean Sea. He was a beautiful baby, well formed with clear and soft features—not the rough blurred lines of the typical newly-born infant.

"Walking through the fields and carrying him in my arms. He was so light and gurgled and cooed endlessly.

"Pushing him down the street in his baby carriage. People stopped to look at him. Comments on how beautiful he was.

"He was about three years old. One fourth-of-July night I sat on the sidewalk with him on my lap. He was in his pajamas. He shrieked with delight as we watched the fireworks being shot into the sky.

"When he was six years old, I took him to school for the

children's program. He was dressed in a little suit with a bow-tie. He was adorable, and I had this loving, melting feeling of joy that he gave me by his very existence."

Such strong emotional feelings of a loving father tend to insure a caring attitude that is beneficial to both father and son. In most cases this loving bond produces a caring lifestyle for both father and son. Despite the dominant positive characteristics of this type of father, some caveats about the loving-father style are in order. Love does not always conquer all.

A son is not totally influenced by his father, no matter how loving or compassionate he may be. There are peers, mother, siblings and community influences which can negatively affect the socialization process. Although a loving father may block and help resolve many of his son's problems, it is not always possible for him to counter all negative impacts.

I have observed that some loving fathers, in their attempt to block all negative influences, envelop their sons in a blanket of dependency. This problem arises when such fathers become overloving, overcompassionate and overdoubling.

A father of this type can have a negative impact on his son by overprotecting him from the pain of failure, the experience of which is important in the process of growth. The doubling father seldom admits his son has failed at anything, because to do so is to admit he too has failed. He may tell his son everything is okay even when it isn't. Failing and losing are experiences that everyone must learn to deal with effectively. But the son of the overdoubling father may never learn to cope with these normal experiences, because his father absorbs all of life's punches for him. The consequence of this well-intentioned father style is the encapsulation of the son in a warm and loving but unrealistic cocoon.

For example, one man I interviewed loved his son so much he reacted to all his son's failures with complete compassion and support. When his son failed a course in school, he would let him know it didn't matter. "I know how smart you are—the teacher must be an idiot." His overcaring attitude involved providing his son with every luxury that a child of his age could have. Bikes, then motorcycles, cars and expense money, etc., were all provided without any input or effort by the child. The child swam in all of this opulence and unconditional love—and almost drowned. When he encountered more realistic responses from the world at large he felt anger at these people who were playing the game of life by a different rule—"You get when you give." Because of his father's total acceptance he was unable to cope with the real world.

Another way in which the overinvolved doubling father can negatively affect his son is by unwittingly setting up unattainable goals. Because his father is so accepting, the son loves him in return and wants to please him. The child becomes overly concerned with the doubling father's pleasure and pain over his successes and failures in school, sports or with his friends. As a result of this overidentification with his father, the child in his effort to make his father feel good will press too hard to succeed, and because he is under enormous pressure, he will often fail.

For example, I have observed in children's sports competition that the macho father, who openly yells at his ball-playing son for making an error or striking out, may have less of a negative impact on his son than an overloving-doubling father. The macho father is *open* about his displeasure, and the child can sometimes learn to deal with the situation. In the case of the overloving-doubling father, the child identifies with his empathetic father, who suffers for him and with him every time he fails.

It's hard for the father and son to rationalize a strike-out or an error when everyone at the game reacts negatively. The father and son become locked into pleasing each other. The father may feel pain because his son has struck out, and the son often feels guilty about causing his father pain. He begins to "press" on the field (or in life) because he senses that a strike-out or an error hurts his father.

The doubling father who openly loves his child too much may, like the classic "Yiddishe momma," so overwhelm his son and smother him that the child fails because of the tremendous pressure he is constantly experiencing. The fanatically doubling father loves his son but his smothering behavior doesn't permit his son to achieve his own identity, or to learn how to cope with the real world.

2. *Peer-Type Fathers: Buddies* Many overloving-doubling fathers become buddies rather than fathers to their sons. Such men do not assume the proper status of fathers because they do not perceive themselves as superordinate to anyone, or capable of controlling anyone. They remain boys or son-types no matter what their age. They attempt to be "buddies" or peers with their sons rather than fathers. Emotionally, they are perpetual children who have not attained sufficient maturity to become fathers.

Such a father may love his son like a brother, but because of his peership behavior he doesn't generate much respect from his son, nor does he offer much of a lofty role model for his son to emulate.

Peer fathers usually feel besieged by their problems and the world around them and are not motivated toward heavy achievements. They tend to share their problems with their sons. In this way they often place unnecessary burdens on their sons at too early an age. They seldom discipline their sons because they don't have a clear position on correct behavior or rules. They are usually dominated by their wives and only serve as agents of their wives in the control and discipline of their sons.

My own father was in this category. He always shared his problems with his sons, thus burdening them with a gloom-and-doom vision of the world. When my father disciplined me, it was only after he had been harassed by my mother to "do something" about me. Then he would in effect tell me my bad behavior (whatever it was) didn't really matter to him. But it did upset my mother and when she was upset he was in the line of fire. Therefore, he told me to "straighten up and fly right" not because of any correct-behavior precepts he held, but because my mother was giving him trouble. In many ways he was not a father figure, but a beaten-down older brother who was another child to my mother.

His role as a "brother" who was unwilling to be my superior was revealed to me in a recent comment: "You know, Lewie, you don't remember, but sometimes when your mother was going to hit you or one of the other boys, I would say, 'Don't hit them, hit me first.' "

A positive characteristic of peer-buddy fathers is that many of them tend to be playmates to their sons. They can sometimes be "good brothers" who supply a friendship that is denied to sons of competitive or macho fathers. My father and I had many positive memorable times together playing baseball. I think he wished he could play with me on my high school team, because he seldom missed a game.

A psychologist I interviewed described his own buddy-father as "a man who had no balls at all. He was always puling, whining and complaining about life. My mother totally dominated him. He would only discipline us at her behest. His heart wasn't in it because he had little concern with bringing us up. He was so embittered by his plight in the world. I had the feeling he was always jealous of me because I was the youngest one in the family. I believed he longed to be the kid brother, because that would automatically get him more affection from our mom. He could then relax and not have to fight the world as hard. He wanted to be one of my mother's sons, not a father."

3. *Macho Fathers* Macho fathers have an exaggerated idea of the meaning of masculinity. This type of father basically relates to his son as an extension of his own ego, and in effect is little concerned from a compassionate viewpoint with his son's ego development. The extreme macho father is a man whose personal masculinity and identity is tied to his son's performance, as it relates to his own egocentric needs.

Although fathers of this type are not necessarily physically battering fathers, most brutal fathers tend to fall into this category. Their brutality occurs more often on a subtly emotional verbal level than on a physical level. They are superdirectors of their sons' lives, and their sons seldom develop any personal autonomy, because their fathers' superman judgmental postures are omnipresent.

A big-league ballplayer revealed to me how most of his lifelong problems developed from his conflict with his domineering macho father. The father succeeded in making him into a great big-league baseball star at the expense of the son's emotional health. The star ballplayer wound up in several mental hospitals, largely as a result of his father's excessive motivation for success and the brutal demands he made on his son.

Essentially, the macho father seldom permits his son to become an individual in his own right. He goes through life as an ego extension of his macho father, in the shadow of his father —for his father's aggrandizement. The son's ego is dwarfed by the father's self-glorification.

My research reveals that sons of macho fathers develop three types of personality formations as a response to the father's treatment: (1) a *carbon copy* son, who has totally capitulated to the father through emulation; (2) an *openly rebellious* son, who reacts negatively to almost everything his father stands for and wants him to become; and (3) a *passive-aggressive* son, who obeys all orders but seethes with hostility underneath his passive exterior.

In a newspaper interview, General Patton's son, George S. Patton, Jr., revealed his extreme level of carbon copy identification with his famous father. In one segment of the interview, the general's son described a vision he had in battle in which his father's image appeared to give him direction.

" 'I pressed my body against the Korean earth as shrapnel from the Chinese artillery shattered the ground around me. My radio, the only means of getting ammunition for the platoons, was 50 yards away, across a road. I had to get some ammunition to 'em. They were screaming for it. It was unbelievable . . . just a storm of steel coming down. I was shaking like a leaf. I looked up at the sky and I said, "What the hell should I do?" Then I saw him just as plain as day. He said, "Get on across the road. It's your duty." I got up and crossed myself a couple of times and I mean to tell you, I've never seen anything like it. As I got about in the middle of the road, the firing stopped. Just for a second. And I'll never forget that.' "

The image and voice that answered his frightened plea was unmistakably seen by the son as that of his late father, the colorful and sometimes outrageous World War II general who became a military folk hero. Patton told how, as a young man, he wrote to his father and asked the general how he could avoid showing cowardice. His father replied, "Your blood won't let you."

68

"Like his father during a training mission in Germany, he found himself at a spot where a Napoleonic battle had been fought. He was overcome with a feeling, such as the ones experienced by his father, that he once had been in combat there himself. His father had written of experiencing déjà vu several times. He believed he had served in France as a member of a Roman legion and later as a knight in the Crusades."[4]

Patton, Jr., rejects the suggestion that he is "a chip off the old block." However, in addition to his belief in reincarnation, there are striking similarities between father and son in many areas of their lives. Both went to West Point. Both flunked mathematics. Both were tossed out of the academy because of it. Both crammed for and then passed the reentry exam. (The son attended West Point thirty-eight years after the father.) Both men commanded the Second Armored Division, the only division in Army history commanded by a father and son.

The power of General Patton, a macho father, enveloped his son's personality. There seemed to be no in-between response to such a strong and clear personality, who was so powerfully dedicated to his occupation. The son either could become like his father or totally rebel. His only assertion of selfdom appeared to be in the change of his name from George Patton IV to George S. Patton, Jr.

The second response—overt rebellion—occurs when a son, usually in his late-teen to early adult years, takes the position opposite to his father's in all areas, including social, economic and political. Many sons of macho fathers rebelled in the late 1960s. They seized their historic moment to become hippies, ran away from home, and lived in "crash pads" in places like Haight-Ashbury or in communes, as an act of rebellion against their uptight macho fathers.

I am convinced that some rebellious sons develop a homosexual preference as a reaction against their super-macho fathers. One macho father I interviewed was convinced of this. He remarked, "I know my son became a sissy queer because he knows how much I detest them. It was an act of spite. I'm sure of it."

Certainly homosexuality is a more complex phenomenon than is revealed by this simple analysis. However, in some cases it is true that a son's homosexuality can be a rebellious reaction-formation to the demand for super-macho behavior by a macho father.

Interestingly, a macho father's hopes for his son's excessive masculinity can lead to a no-win situation. If the son is less macho or manly than the father, the latter is disappointed; and if the son surpasses his father's masculinity, the macho father is defeated by his own son. In either case his hopes are not fulfilled, and he loses.

A third response to a macho father is to become passive-aggressive. The son, overtly appearing to conform to his father's control, actually seethes with rebellious, hostile emotions under the surface. In this context a son I interviewed, whose macho father was a construction worker, commented as follows about his macho father's influence on his personality.

"My father did not talk to me very much. Instead of talking he would beat me frequently and severely when, in his words, 'I wasn't a real man.' I began to wish he would die so he could not beat me any more. He told me beatings were good for me and would toughen me. He told me they would make a man out of me. Instead he succeeded in terrorizing me. I've gone through life frightened and unsure of myself. I have lost several jobs because of my terror of authority figures and I've been trying to work my problem out in therapy."

I have had many therapeutic sessions with sons who become victims of this type of response to their controlling, overbearing "be-a-man" macho fathers. The following detailed psychodrama session reflects a son's prototypical reaction to his macho father. (I will present the dynamics of this session in considerable detail with two purposes in mind. One is to reveal a son's passive-aggressive response to his macho father's impact, and secondly, since I refer to psychodrama sessions throughout the book, this protocol of a session may be used to reveal some of the procedures involved in the method.)[5]

The session took place with a group of ten men who had agreed to focus on their father-son relationships from the sons' points of view. After a preliminary discussion of various types of fathers, the members of the group discussed their own fathers, their feelings about them and how they were affected by them.

70

A young, mild-mannered man told the group he was unsure about how he really felt about his father, but he was convinced that his father was a macho man and had had quite a negative influence on him and his lifestyle. I asked him to come up on stage and explain himself to the group in more detail. (This self-presentation is important to almost every session in order to tune the group and the protagonist into the protagonist's self-concept.) He said, "My name is Dan and I'm twenty-five. I work in an office as a clerk. I dropped out of college; it was just too hard for me. I'm alone. I would like to have a girlfriend but I'm too shy and unsure of myself. I don't think I'm man enough for most women. My father has badgered me all my life to 'be a man.' I'm a big disappointment to him. I left home last year against my father's wishes. He and I simply never could talk to each other, and he made my life hell."

We go to the scene when he leaves home. An older member of the group who has a son Dan's age volunteers to play the role of Dan's father. It becomes apparent as the session unfolds that Dan's basic life conflict is with his macho father. We note that as he talks to the man playing his father in the session, he is overtly obedient, repeatedly saying "Yes, sir," but on the body level, he clenches his fists so tightly his knuckles are white. His "father" storms around, essentially telling him in different ways, "You're a little baby, a sissy. You can't make it in the world without my support. Therefore, you'll do exactly as I say."

Dan is then directed to reverse roles with his "father."

L.Y.: You are now your dad. How old a man are you?

DAN AS FATHER: Fifty-four.

L.Y.: What's your name?

DAN AS FATHER: Dan.

L.Y.: No, you are now your father. What's your name? [Our purpose here is to get him into the role of his father as much as possible, in order to better understand his father's viewpoint.]

DAN AS FATHER: Roy.

L.Y.: Does anyone in the group want to ask Roy here a question?

GROUP MEMBER: Do you love your son?

71

DAN AS FATHER: I say I do, but I never show it. I don't know how. My father [Dan's grandfather] never showed me any affection either.

G.M.: Why don't you love your son?

DAN AS FATHER: First of all, get one thing straight. I never wanted the little bastard. She [Roy's wife] trapped me into this marriage by purposely getting knocked up. My son Dan's a puny little shit. I wanted my son to be an athlete, someone with balls. He's a sissy.

I now have Dan return to his own role. He is visibly shaken by the pronouncements which he, in the role of his father, has made about himself.

L.Y.: Okay, Dan. Here's your father again. [The older man returns to play the role of his father.] Tell him what you really think of him.

DAN (*red-faced, almost sobbing*): I can't. He's twice my size and he'll beat me up if I say the wrong thing to him. I'm always scared of him.

The group and the director become aware of the disparity between Dan's perception of his father and reality. Dan is six foot three, but he still perceives his real father (who we later find out is only six feet tall) from a little boy's perspective.

L.Y.: I'm going to put in another Dan as a double to help you encounter your father.

I select a member of the group who is well over six feet and weighs around 200 pounds. He stands beside Dan and his purpose as a double is to help Dan stand up to his father. The conversation continues with the "father" berating Dan as "little Danny," a "punk" and a "sissy." Dan and his double are acting obedient toward the father, as Dan did in the real-life situation. The person playing the father imitates Dan and emits exaggeratedly obedient "Yes, sirs," which the real Dan, red-faced, repeats subserviently. Dan's clenched fists and body posture belie the obedient son he is overtly playing. The real Dan is obviously seething with rage toward his father underneath the polite remarks he is making.

At this point I surreptitiously ask the double to attempt to bring out Dan's real underlying feelings of hostility toward his father. Dan's double then blurts out: "I hate your fuckin' guts. You son of a bitch, I can't stand you anymore—you're driving me nuts!"

As the double apparently brings to the surface Dan's real feelings, the real Dan opens up and begins to lunge at the man playing his father. Animal grunts and screams emerge from Dan's body. He holds on to his "father's" throat. (Psychodramatically the "throat" is a rolled-up newspaper held in position by the auxiliary ego playing the father.) Dan is now experiencing his real feelings toward his father, and he continues for several minutes to groan and sob with pain.

I give the man playing Dan's father a pillow to hold in front of him, and Dan is told:

L.Y.: Okay, you can hit him.
DAN: I can't hit my father. I'm afraid of him.
L.Y.: First of all, this is not really your father, so you can't hurt *him*. Also, I guarantee that this man playing your father will not hit you back. A thing we can do in psychodrama is determine the size and shape of your hostility. You've been carrying these unexpressed feelings of hostility toward your father around with you all your life. Now you have an opportunity to experience the intensity of these negative feelings you have about your father. All of us here want to help you. [The group expresses their involvement with Dan and their desire to help.]

At first Dan begins to viciously punch the pillow held by the man playing his father. He starts to cry. As he continues to physically act out his rage, he almost begins to enjoy it. After his years of pent-up anger toward his father have been exorcised, he begins to smile, and he says, "I really want to choke the bastard." He then chokes the pillow still held by the auxiliary ego playing the role of his father.

Now that most of his anger has been expelled, I attempt to

73

focus Dan's session and move from Dan's catharsis of hostility into some personal insights.

L.Y.: Okay. Now I want you to punch the pillow again as if it were your father. But with each punch, I want you to state why you're punching him.
   (Dan throws a hard punch.)
L.Y.: What's that for?
DAN: For never wanting me as your son!
   (Another punch.)
L.Y.: What's that for?
DAN: For making fun of me when I was a kid and calling me a sissy.
   (Another punch.)
L.Y.: What's that for?
DAN: For the times you got drunk and beat up on my mother.
   [Dan is now more in control of his emotions as he methodically reviews the basic reasons for his hostility toward his father.]
   (Another punch.)
L.Y.: What's that for?
DAN: For being ashamed of me and not taking me anywhere.
   [This goes on with several other formerly repressed complaints being brought to the surface. Now that Dan's anger and hostility have been dispelled, I encourage Dan to express some of his positive attitudes toward his father.]
L.Y. *(to the man playing Dan's father)*: Okay, hug your son.
DAN: I don't want him to do it.
L.Y.: Yes you do. See what it feels like.
   (The man playing Dan's father hugs Dan and Dan breaks into tears again in his psychodramatic "father's" arms.)
DAN: Dad, that's what I always wanted from you—just for you to love me and tell me I'm okay. You never held me like this before.
"FATHER": I've always loved you, son, but I never learned how to express it. Can you forgive me?
DAN: I don't know.
L.Y. AND GROUP: Why don't you forgive him?

74

DAN: I'll try, but I'm not sure I can do it.

L.Y.: If you can really forgive him, you'll also give up that ball of hostility in your gut that you have from hating him all these years. You will free yourself from being entrapped by your anger. You accept the self-doubt and low self-concept generated by your father. He has, because of his own needs and problems, carried on a false propaganda campaign against you all your life. He defined you as a sissy because you didn't act like he wanted you to. We see you as a fine man who has been victimized by your authoritarian father. You can rise above the problem by understanding how your grandfather probably made your father enact his life role in that tough macho style. You can break this negative chain in your family by understanding it and becoming a loving compassionate father to your own son when you have one.

Several young men in the group come on stage to express their feelings toward their fathers, with other members of the group playing the necessary father role. Using Dan's experience, they quickly get to the center of their problems with their fathers. This part of the session is most important, as it provides the opportunity for other members of the group to express their emotions. As he sees the similarities to his own session, Dan now understands that he is not alone with his problem, and this is also useful to him.

Another group member, Todd, who participated in Dan's session as his double, appears warmed up to a "mini-session" of his own. In fact, Todd is a good double for Dan because his emotions reflecting his own life situation are very close to those felt by Dan. With auxiliary egos I set the scene for Todd to give him the opportunity to violently act out his pent-up frustration and anger, and the pain he feels about his own macho father. At this point I hand him a battoca (the cushionlike weapon used in group sessions to express anger) so he can pound out the rage he has felt but never expressed toward his father. Todd takes the battoca but doesn't use it. He explains his feelings to the man playing his father as follows:

"I was just a little kid. Why did you have to beat me up all the time? I never even did anything wrong. And you used to hit my mother too, for no good reason. You were always drunk and mean, and if it wasn't for my mom we wouldn't even have had food in the house. I was just marking time until I was old enough and big enough to beat the shit out of you like you did to us, and then you got sick. How can I be so angry with you when I feel sorry for you? You're a sick man who's now bedridden." Turning to the group, Todd continues: "How can I say anything mean or angry to a man who's sick with a heart condition? He always screams at my mother to bring him this and bring him that and then berates her. He'd attack us personally, tell us we were ugly and no good. He was full of bitterness and took it out on us. But my mom always apologized for him and told us if we said one word against him we'd be sorry, because upsetting him might shorten his life. I can't hit him or yell at him even here, now. I feel too guilty, too sorry for him, or at least that's the trip my mother laid on me. Everything now revolves around 'poor Daddy,' and I'm stuck with all these feelings of rage."

Dan tells Todd how he feels much better since he acted out his rage against his father in the session. With Dan's, the group's and my support, Todd beats on his psychodramatic father with the battoca. He really cuts loose, expressing much of his pent-up rage and venom. He concludes by telling the group that he feels better now that he has expressed his rage.

The first protagonist, Dan, obviously stirred up many negative feelings in the group toward their fathers. There were, of course, some who indicated that their fathers were loving and caring and they had no problems with them.

At this point, the group was prepared for a more generalized analysis of the session, and I delineated the following points about dealing with hostile feelings against macho fathers.

Dan went through four typical phases that appear in many sessions when a son breaks through into expressing his hostility and the pain he has felt because he found it necessary to suppress his real feelings toward his macho father: Phase I—the recognition of the size and shape of his hostility; Phase II—cathartic acting out of hostility toward parental object of pain; Phase III—expression of primal pain (nonverbal groans and crying) that in a sense mourns the felt absence of desired parental love; and Phase IV—forgiveness and possible expression of love.

In Phase I the protagonist locates and recognizes his enormous pent-up hostility about long-term grievances. The group and the psychodrama director, through a double, often find it necessary to explicate the protagonist's grievances.

Following this, Phase II should give the protagonist the opportunity to specifically express his rage for the many years of pain. The protagonist, by punching a pillow, using a battoca, kicking or whatever form his venom takes, will typically express his hostility in a torrent of anger. Curiously, everyone seems to harbor his own personal pattern of expressing his anger. For most, the pillow or battoca is fine, but some people want to use poison, a gun or other forms of destruction.

In this phase of expression, it is important to have the protagonist express his explicit grievances. As Dan said, with each punch, "This is for not wanting me . . . this is for never approving of anything I did. . . ." etc. This process helps the protagonist to understand more clearly the inadequacies that have been projected onto him and the degree to which he has accepted this propaganda, which usually results in self-hatred and a low self-concept.

At this point, entering Phase III, the protagonist begins to feel his deeper pain and typically cry and groan with deep emotion. It is important to let him experience his pain and not cut off his expression prematurely by soothing him. It is necessary for the protagonist to take as much time as he needs for this phase, with the father (auxiliary ego) present.

Phase IV, the expression of love and forgiveness, does not usually emerge in most sessions as readily as the earlier expression of hostility. My experience reveals that this phase of forgiveness and affection can seldom be fully expressed (except superficially) *until* the protagonist has *first* fully expressed his feelings of hostility toward his father. Once this has happened, however, the protagonist is in a position to forgive and try to forget. As the director, I always emphasize that the symbolic and sometimes real expression of forgiveness is not for the benefit of the father but should provide relief for the protagonist. When he can forgive, he divests himself of the necessity of carrying around his rage and maintaining a vendetta that more often than not impairs his happiness and produces self-defeating behavior patterns.

Occasionally, a protagonist can experience these four phases in one session. It is more likely, however, that the full experience will take place through a number of psychodramatic experiences (which may be combined with individual therapeutic sessions). It is usually necessary to be the central protagonist in at least one session in order to go through this pattern of self-liberation; however, it should be emphasized that people can achieve some (or even all) facets of this experience by deep involvement in sessions with other protagonists who are going through the process. Therefore, a person can benefit from psychodrama not only from the position of protagonist but also from being an actively involved group member.

The session presented here detailed the complexity of rage that can develop in the dominated son of a macho father. Various father styles produce their special affects on a son's personality. A father style that produces even more problems for a son than that of the macho father is the psychopathic father style. .

4. *The Psychopathic Father* The dominant personality factor of the psychopathic father is his basic lack of compassion. It is regrettable when a psychopathic man has a child, because as a father he is incapable of training that child to feel human. He is at the opposite extreme from a compassionate loving-doubling father.

By definition, the psychopathic personality exhibits a persistent behavior pattern characterized by an almost total disregard for the rights and feelings of others. A listing of psychopathic personality and behavior traits includes most, if not all, of the following factors: (1) a limited social conscience; (2) an egocentrism dominating most interaction and instrumental manipulation of others for self-advantage (rather than effective relating); (3) an inability to forgo immediate pleasure for future goals; and (4) a habit of pathological lying to achieve personal advantage.

The dominant theme of the psychopathic personality is what has varyingly been called "moral imbecility" or "character disorder." This type of personality may know right from wrong, but a dominating theme of his behavior is that he lacks any coherent ability to discriminate between them in his actions. In brief, the distinction between right and wrong doesn't really matter to the psychopath. He has a moral or character disorder. A simple definition of the psychopath is that he has a condition of psychological abnormality in which there is neither the overt appearance of psychosis nor of neurosis, but where there is a chronic abnormal response to the environment. A psychopathic person is insensitive to social demands; he either refuses to or cannot cooperate socially. Psychopaths are untrustworthy, impulsive and improvident. They show poor judgment, shallow emotionality, and seem unable to comprehend the reason for negative reactions of others to their behavior.

A basic personality defect of the psychopath is a limited social conscience toward almost all others to whom he relates, of course including his sons. This characteristic is most apparent in the psychopath's limited feelings of real sympathy for others or regret for the harm he does them.

A dominant feature of the psychopathic father is his *lack* of real interest in his son's growth and development, even though he may feign an interest. Following is a portrait of such a father as described in an interview with his son.

"My father is handsome and bears a slight resemblance to Clark Gable. He was a talented actor, writer and director, and had appeared in and directed several plays in small playhouses throughout New York. He also conducted a drama class. His present occupation is making pornographic films. He has his own company, and he writes, produces and directs the films and has appeared in them himself.

"I can't think of anything positive about him. The negative events I remember were his physical fights with my mother. He beat up Mom—it was traumatic. She moved to Europe and I saw my dad with another woman shortly thereafter. This bothered me and made me angry. I was thirteen years old at the time.

"I was closer to Mom than to my dad. The first twelve years of my life Dad was distant. My relationship with my father went downhill when he was involved with another woman. Dad is incapable of showing positive emotions. What he can show is violence. He always told me I'd fail. He disciplined me by hitting me with a belt or beating me up.

"The amount and quality of time my father spent with me was almost zero. He was selfish in every way [egocentric]. When my mom left my dad and went to Europe, I stayed with my dad. I was left alone with no supervision while he was busy working at the theater. He fell short of being a father because of his selfishness, and he also lied to me a lot. He never knew how to give or to show affection. I wish he had spent more time with me. Even if I needed something, he did not have the money for me, only for himself. He really was a model of a totally self-centered person. I never wanted to become like him, but I see now that I am like him in many ways."

A tendency toward administering intense, often erratic discipline is one of the characteristics of the psychopathic father. One young man described his psychopathic father's discipline approach to me as follows:

"I cannot recall any peak events in my life with my father that were positive. All of my peak events with him were negative. These events centered around discipline. My father's disciplinary techniques were very violent and for the most part physical. For example, one incident that will always stick out in my mind was the time when I was five years old and I lost a dollar. My father reacted as though I had lost a million dollars. After screaming for an hour about how stupid and irresponsible I was, he ended up by hitting me in the head with a board!

"My father had a self-centered outlook on life. I always wanted a father who was guiding and instructive, someone who would come home from work every day and talk about what had happened, ask me what was new, care about me. I would have liked my father to treat me as a friend and not as an object, which was the way he treated me. My father did not guide me the right way. His advice was never given in an affectionate or loving manner. He was clearly uninvolved and self-centered. He was uninvolved in my everyday life. My father gave me little emotional support."

Many young men who have psychopathic fathers like the type described seek out surrogate fathers. Some are lucky to have a teacher, stepfather, coach or employer who presents a more compassionate and logical role model. Sons with negative psychopathic fathers are vulnerable to the influence of "positive image" psychopathic fathers. Cult leaders and pseudoreligious leaders fit this model. They seem to be manifestly "good" fathers because they preach a positive gospel, even though they too are basically self-centered psychopaths. Their appearance to the world as humanitarian, caring fathers sets up an irresistible attraction for sons of more obvious psychopaths. An example of this type of surrogate psychopathic father was the Reverend Jim Jones.

Most people turn to God for positive reasons. However, some sons who have psychopathic macho fathers turn to God as a substitute father. One man interviewed described this process in the following way:

"My father was extremely uninvolved, and never seemed to spend any time with me at all. When he did see me, he tended to be very competitive. I would have loved to have him come and watch me perform in ski-jump races and gymnastic tournaments. *No one came to watch me.* My real father was very important to me only because he gave me a model that I can avoid following. I don't want to fuck up like he did. I would have played more games with drugs, but was afraid of becoming addicted and weak like my father, who became an alcoholic. He was a good negative model for me.

"The only father I admire is God. I call God 'Father.' God *is* my father. The Reverend J.F. is my spiritual God also. He is the head of a church in Los Angeles. As a child I was not religious at all and neither were my parents. But now I have a father, *the* Father."

5. *The Egocentric Father* My research reveals two types of psychopathic father styles. The one type described exists where the father's *personality* is psychopathic. This type of man clearly enacts his role in a manifestly charming, often charismatic, yet egocentric, manner. He performs the father role in this fashion because that's the way he is, and his behavior merely reflects his psychopathic personality.

However, there are men with relatively normal personalities

81

who are *situational psychopathic fathers,* and in effect they treat their sons coldly, without compassion. I would characterize the egocentric father as a man who acts in a psychopathic way because of his response to his life circumstances in a competitive society, rather than as a reflection of a basically psychopathic personality.

In earlier times a son could be a functional unit and an economic asset to his father. He would maintain the family name or business, and provide the means for helping his father financially in his old age. In contemporary society, however, a father is forced to spend money on his child early in his career, when he could use all of his time and money to further his strivings for success.

Because of this situation in our competitive society, a son can become a block to the father's drive for success. In his professional life the egocentric father rapidly learns to perceive people as objects to be manipulated in his striving for success. The same manipulative techniques that he has cultivated in his occupational situation cannot simply be abandoned when he leaves his workplace. His unsympathetic approach to people as objects in the marketplace of life extends to his family relationships. His son, in this context, can become someone who hinders rather than aids his drive for upward mobility. To the egocentric father, even his wife is seen as a helpful or harmful entity in his quest toward the holy grail of success.

The egocentric father is not necessarily a cold person, but his competitive stance toward the world in general seems vital to him in the society he lives in. "Winning through intimidation," "looking out for Number One" or "by whatever means necessary" are the guiding themes for his behavior.

Men who assume this general social-emotional stance because of the economic realities of their life tend to act toward their sons in the same way they respond to the world around them. Their sons' time and needs are in competition with the time and energy they require for success, wealth and power in their own lives. "Time is money" in this social configuration, and time spent with their sons is in competition with their egocentric success orientation.

At different points in time his life situation tends to produce a basic role conflict in this type of father. He has the capacity to and may want to enact his loving-father role and give to his son. On the other hand, doing that will mean that he has less time to fulfill his need to succeed. Which role will take precedence? The egocentric father can always rationalize his self-serving role by telling himself that if he is more successful he will be of greater help to his son in the long run. Also, in the throes of his role conflict, if he opts to center his life or time on his son, he may instill guilt in the boy by letting him know that he is taking time from "more important matters" to be with him. By doing this he will corrupt the quality of the time he spends with his son. Most fathers at some point in their relationships with their sons have to resolve this role conflict in both specific situations and over the totality of their father-son relationships.

As a result of this socioeconomic drag factor, the father develops a certain degree of ambivalence toward his child. He feels, consciously or unconsciously, an ambivalence, because he has positive feelings for the child, yet he is aware that his love object partially blocks his drive toward success. The egocentric father may turn on his son in various ways, including giving him abnormal amounts of disapproval as a response to his ambivalent feelings. His response may negatively affect the son's self-esteem and personality development. These negative actions may be covertly acted out by the egocentric father. He may carefully project a model loving-father image to the world, despite the fact that he feels plagued by a son who impedes his professional goals.

In brief, many men in our society tend to become competitive, exploitative persons who view others not humanistically but as objects, or as means toward the end of upward mobility in the American success syndrome. This perception of the world often involves a callous, coldblooded, manipulative attitude toward one's own family and in effect produces an egocentric father.

Celebrity fathers are apt to be egocentric fathers. If they are not egocentric when they begin their careers, they are likely to become that way as a result of the enormous adulation they receive from the public. Since they are in such great demand, most of them have some level of guilt because they usually have insufficient time in their busy schedules to give quality time to their sons. They may rationalize their guilt away by telling themselves, as one celebrity father told me, "I'm doing this largely for my family." In fact, most celebrity fathers are geared toward doing whatever is necessary, by whatever means necessary, to maintain their position on the mountain of success. Unless they take the time that is vital to nurture their family relationships (as many do), they are prone to enacting the egocentric-father role with their sons.

Wealthy upper-socioeconomic-class men are also likely to become egocentric fathers because of their positions of power in the world. Many perceive their sons as part of their holdings and consequently take a cold emotional stance toward them when the sons require their time and support. They often treat their sons as part of their property, rather than with the love and attention their sons need.

In this context, I recall the case of a very wealthy father who clearly enacted the egocentric-father role with his son. He had recently divorced, and afterwards coldly ignored his son who he felt impeded fulfillment of his egocentric needs for personal success and his newly developed swinger self-image. He didn't want his son with him because he felt the boy would get in his way. His ex-wife, because of her personal problems, couldn't be of help. The forty-five-year-old sharply attired swinger decided his son could not live with him because it would cramp his style with his newly acquired young live-in mistress. He had the affluence to plant his "emotionally disturbed" son in a foster home.

For a time my wife and I took in some such displaced youngsters during their crisis periods with their parents, and this boy was one. I have never forgotten my interview with this father, and how he openly detailed his self-centered reasons for abandoning his son.

I found one part of our conversation particularly obnoxious. I felt the boy would benefit if he went to a certain private school while he lived with us. The father said, "I don't have any money in the budget for my son for that. He'll have to go to public school." The man refused to contribute anything to his son's education. After much haggling, I finally agreed to lower my fairly spartan monthly fee, which was to cover the boy's needs while he stayed in my home, so that he could go to private school.

When our business was completed, he said, "Come outside with me. I want to show you something nice." It turned out he wanted to show me the new Rolls-Royce he had bought for 100,000 dollars that day. His self-image clearly took precedence over his father role to the detriment of his son's emotional condition. The man was a prototypical egocentric father who, like many American men in every echelon, was consumed by his own needs for personal validation through extravagant self-centered success, in this case at the expense of his son's personal development. The father was a real estate supersalesman, a profession that fits easily into the egocentric-father model. A typical salesman adopts a gracious patina of compassion for his client, but in reality he would readily sell the proverbial Eskimo a refrigerator. Can such a salesman, who spends eight or more hours a day viewing clients as objects to be exploited, using situational ethics, lying if need be, and manipulating his client for the basic goal of sales-seduction, change his stance with his son and family? My observation is that most fathers who play this hustler role in their jobs have difficulty switching over to the role of honestly compassionate, loving fathers during the brief periods they spend with their sons.

There are too many egocentric fathers in our society. This type of father, consumed by his quest for upward mobility, like Abraham sacrifices his son to our society's apocryphal God of success. Psychopathic fathers seldom change; however, egocentric fathers can be converted into loving, compassionate fathers. A key to change is a self-recognition of their problem.

FATHER-TYPE AND SON-TYPE MEN

A man's style of fathering obviously has significant impacts on his son's basic personality and approach to life. Because of their fathers, some sons approach life with joy and zest. Others, those who are in search of fathers, become locked in self-defeating competitive struggles with their fathers and other men.

A most significant result of the father's impact on his son will be the son's tendency to become either a *father type* or a *son type* personality. By this I mean that men go through life predominantly playing father or son roles in all their relationships. (To son types, their wives are really "mommies.")

To become an effective father type, a man has to develop many positive characteristics, including inner strength, independence and leadership qualities. He becomes a person who has in some measure become self-actualized. Some males never grow out of playing the son role in life. Such men seldom become positive father figures to their children, and they tend to play a second-string role in all of their life occupations. Son-types are usually dependent, require considerable and constant nurturing, have limited leadership qualities and are "other-directed" in most of their relationships. When they become fathers, they usually turn out to be weak peer-buddy fathers who tend to produce a second generation of weak sons.

A number of speculative hypotheses are in order on this issue. One is that a man will assume a father-type role in life at an early age because of the absence of a strong father figure in his life. In a sense he becomes his own father. This often occurs in families where the biological father is not physically present because of abandonment, divorce or death. Here a son is forced to assume an adult father role early in life. A component of becoming a father type in this context may be a mother who projects this role onto the oldest son. In brief, a family needs a male father figure and the son, even though he's only ten or fifteen, must undertake this role. In a sense he is drafted by the family for the father role. Young men of this type tend to become strong fathers in later life to their own sons, because they had to assume the father role at an early age.

Sons with strong, ever-present, loving fathers may assume a father role in life gracefully because they admire and respect their own fathers, and consequently find the role desirable. They want to emulate their fathers because they see them as having a happy, fulfilling lifestyle. Simply stated, the father is a positive role model and the son wants to become like him.

In contrast, sons with egocentric, psychopathic or macho cruel fathers may remain perpetual sons because they do not want to become father types. Their unconscious reasoning is "If that's what a father is like, I don't want to become a father!" Also, their situation does not provide a good role model to learn the father role from. Because they cannot identify with their negative macho or competitive fathers, they do not learn how to become effective fathers and they tend to remain son-types.

Most psychopathic criminals are son-types, and become bad fathers. Criminals of this type, even those who tattoo their bodies in macho ways to compensate for their childlike state, are basically angry, childlike son-types. They continuously defy father figures and refuse to properly assume a father role in life. Prison is an appropriate place for rebellious son-type men who hate authority. Criminals go through life struggling against authority, and in some extreme pathological cases welcome the fatherlike authority of prison officials. Quasi-criminal gangs like the Hell's Angels use the Nazi insignia and admire "heroic" figures like Hitler. They look for a powerful father figure who dominates people as their hero.

Many son-types in this category become seemingly strong (really weak) macho fathers, who keep their sons in servitude as son-types in order to bolster their own masculinity and doubtful sense of their own father status. The son is a "property" that they control and brag about for their own self-aggrandizement. A father of this type is at least in control of someone (his son) for life, but the son of a father of this type is most unlikely to become a father-type man.

Macho, psychopathic, egocentric and peer-buddy fathers produce son-type progeny on the whole, because they do not possess the personalities to transmit real father-type values. In contrast, loving, caring fathers serve as good role models and transmit to their sons the qualities which produce self-actualized men, who in turn themselves become effective father-types.

In summary, a man's father style is determined by the many dynamic factors that affect his personality, especially his own father, who serves as his basic role model. Sons who themselves become forceful, loving father types will have sons who will in turn be good fathers.

With regard to the negative father styles described, changes in their approach can come about only if these fathers become aware of the destructive impact they have on their sons. Only then will they learn to develop more loving father styles. The sons of these fathers do not have to repeat their fathers' sins. Through self-examination and a strong sense of love and compassion for their own sons, they can change the negative impacts of their inheritance from their fathers.

They can begin to revise their negative fathering inheritance during the first phase of the fathering process with their infant sons, and continue the process through the naturally stormy adolescent years. If a father enacts his role properly, one positive result can be a son who becomes a loving best friend when he himself becomes a father-type adult. The revision and reversal of negative father styles over the generations can in effect produce a more loving and compassionate total society.

CHAPTER THREE

The Life Phases of Father-Son Interaction

MARK TWAIN'S PARODY on father-son relationships reveals a deep truth. To paraphrase his comment, "When I was a teenager I thought my father was ignorant. When I was twenty I was amazed at what the old man had learned in a few years."

It is apparent that the relationship between a father and an infant son, and their mutual needs and demands, are considerably different from those between a father and his teenage son, or between a father and his adult son.

In my research, I have observed three basic evolutionary and approximate phases in a typical father-son lifetime relationship: Phase I: ego-blending (birth to twelve years); Phase II: incipient independence and a struggle on the son's part to be his own individual (thirteen to nineteen years); Phase III: man-to-man loving friends (from twenty on).

PHASE I: EGO-BLENDING

In Phase I, ego-blending, a father should have his closest emotional relationship with his son. He should be identified with every facet of ego development from infancy through childhood. Despite the fact that this early nurturing period has been identified as the almost exclusive domain of the mother, there is ample evidence that sons closely watch and react to their fathers, and many fathers closely identify with their sons. This early period should not be the exclusive province of the mother. As foolish macho attitudes are increasingly put aside, and as men begin to emerge as people who can reveal their deeper emotions, fathers can and do become as emotionally close to their sons as mothers are in this early phase.

Fathers who relate to the physical and emotional needs of their young sons on a daily basis tend automatically to merge with the sons' egos and feel with them on a deep emotional level. During this critical phase of self-development a son needs feedback from his father. He looks to his father for approval or disapproval on a daily basis. What his father reflects back to him is the foundation of his self-image as a man.

A son who has a close relationship with his father in this phase is thus constantly examining his own behavior from his father's point of view. Although the boy's mother is important, his father is also a most significant mirror for his developing personality. When my son says, "What do you think, Dad?" about anything, I recognize it as a very serious attempt to assess the situation in question. I am aware that even if he tries to underplay the question, I am playing a very significant role for him when I give him my reaction. Fathers who take this issue lightly, or are indifferent, are doing their sons an enormous disservice, and could have a limiting effect on their sons' self-development.

Naturally, a father need not approve of everything the son says or does, but when his son says, in whatever form the question takes, "What do you think, Dad?" the father should think through his response with great care, for it is the cumulative effect of all these interactions that profoundly influences the son's personality and point of view.

In my own case, the daily contacts I had with my son directly and on the phone, monitoring the events in his life with my wife, were the most profound experiences of my life. And my son has confirmed to me in our recent discussions that he remembers those early experiences with great fondness and appreciation. My doubling or ego-blending with him on a daily basis had a profound effect on his personality.

The ego-blending process is also of great personal significance to the father. A father who immerses himself in this early phase of his son's socialization is bound to become a more humanistic person. His view of the world must necessarily become more compassionate and loving as he consciously observes and participates in the development of his son's self. The process is one of the most profound growth experiences any man can have. It is not a sacrifice or an unpleasant responsibility. It is an experience that should not be missed by any man.

I have observed many formerly cold and distant men who were neglected by their fathers but through their sons were re-socialized into compassionate, loving people. The process of fathering is not a one-way father-to-son street. A son's impact on a father's personality can be very significant. For example, in my research in criminology I have seen many men who were criminals become law-abiding citizens after the birth of a son and their subsequent involvement in his growth.

Fathers who do not ego-blend or double for their sons early on tend to be self-centered, distant fathers. For many sociocultural and historic reasons, the prototypical German father has been a blend of macho and coldness toward his son. A profound negative repercussion of this father style was the emergence in the thirties and forties of a society with a brutal Nazi mentality. Erik Erikson, who carefully studied sociocultural aspects of that period, characterizes the typical Germanic father as follows:

When the Germanic father comes home from work, even the walls seem to pull themselves together ["nehmen sich zu-sammen"]. The mother—although often the unofficial master of the house—behaves differently enough to make a baby aware of it. She hurries to fulfill the father's whims and to avoid angering him. The children hold their breath, for the father does not approve of "nonsense"—that is, neither of the mother's feminine moods nor of the children's playfulness. The mother is required to be at his disposal as long as he is at home; his behavior suggests that he looks with disfavor on that unity of mother and children in which they had indulged in his absence. He often speaks to the mother as he speaks to the children, expecting compliance and cutting off any answer. The little boy comes to feel that all the gratifying ties with his mother are a thorn in the father's side.

The mother increases this feeling by keeping some of the child's "nonsense" or badness from the father—if and when she pleases; while she expresses her disfavor by telling on the child when the father comes home, often making the father execute periodical corporal punishment for misdeeds, the details of which do not interest him. Sons are bad, and punishment is always justified.[1]

German fathers, because of their unique cultural background, manifest a father style that is highly authoritarian and involves severe discipline. The prototypical Germanic father style was revealed to me in an interview I had with a German psychologist and former Luftwaffe pilot who was visiting the United States. His description of several key incidents with his father reflected the generally cold Germanic style of fathering characterized by Erikson.

When Kurt was a child of about sixteen, his father was a Nazi, and an officer in Hitler's army. In 1936, he convinced his son, who was then away at school in Switzerland, to come back to Germany and join Hitler's cause. The young man became a pilot and on his first battle mission was blinded in one eye by shrapnel.

Typically, Kurt was distanced from his Germanic autocratic father. He claimed he respected but never loved his father. He recalled how his father totally dominated him and disciplined him with severe beatings that were part of the disciplinary process of this type of Germanic father style. I asked Kurt to recall the most *pleasant* peak experience he had had with his father, and he told me the following story.

"One day I came home late—I was around nine at the time. Talking to some friends made me late for dinner. Ordinarily my father would take me into a room and beat me with a strap for my offense. I was expecting a beating when I came home. That night for some reason he just shouted at me. Then I'll never forget what he did, and that was over forty years ago. He was drinking some kind of fruit juice. He gave me a sip of the juice and told me to go to my room. I was so overcome by his unusual show of kindness in not beating me that when I was alone in my room I cried uncontrollably."

German fathers of that period are extreme prototypes, but Germany does not have a corner on that type of non-ego-blending father. This type of punitive, distant father exists, more or less, in all cultures—certainly including the United States. This pattern of fathering is not only dehumanizing to the father; it also sets a role-model pattern for the son which unfortunately virtually assures a transmission of its negativity. There is recent research evidence that the prototypical father of the German past has changed in the direction of becoming a more humanistic father figure.

In contrast with this distant, in effect psychopathic, father, the *close doubling* father in this ego-blending phase of relating does something positive for the child. The *close* father teaches his son by his actions the meaning of love, compassion and human warmth; and that these are qualities that a man can and should have. The son will learn how to relate to others in a more humanistic way in later life. He will be able to draw on the doubling experience with his father to develop close relationships with other people. He will have learned through his father's active example how to be compassionate and loving in all his relationships.

The extent to which fathers ego-blend or distance themselves is a key factor in the ethos of a total society. In effect, ego-blending father behavior during the early years of the relationship to a son has a profoundly positive effect on creating a more humanistic social system.

A main deterrent to a father's ego-blending with his son has been the old-fashioned macho attitude. Increasingly, men of today have more appropriate attitudes. As Dr. Herb Goldberg states in his book *The New Male:* "For too long being a socialized man has meant being a well-oiled, predictable, compulsive, controlled performer machine. He blocked out and denied a host of emotions and impulses in himself in order to fit 'comfortably' into harness and to play out the accepted and approved masculine image. The man who becomes suddenly and genuinely self-aware would have to confront and deal with the long-denied responses. The 'new male' is one who can cry and hug his son."[2]

In my book *Robopaths: People as Machines* (Bobbs-Merrill, 1972), I deal with this issue of the macho, psychopathic, distant father. A "robopath" is a person who functions basically as a robot in his relationships. He does what is prescribed by the role he is enacting, and seldom relates in a compassionate and loving manner. In terms of father styles I would characterize him as a hybrid of the egocentric, psychopathic and macho father. His family becomes a kind of social machine because of his behavior. A session I directed with a man who had been this type of father to his son during Phase I of their relationship reveals the impact his behavior had on his son. The session took place when the son was fourteen, and had started to use drugs moderately. The father's enactment in the session was, on the surface, right out of a *Father Knows Best* television drama. He woodenly expressed "compassion" for his son's health, but was more spontaneous and self-righteous in portraying his real concern about the potential irreparable damage to the family's image if the son were ever to be arrested. The father's performance was marked by an almost total lack of truly compassionate emotion toward the son, and the son responded in kind.

After several weeks of sessions the father finally broke out of his macho armor, got down on his knees and poured out fourteen years of repressed tears and emotions he had toward his son. He told him about his beautiful feelings for him when he was born, apologized for seldom spending time with him and expressed great regret that he had not been more compassionate and involved with his son during his early years. He asked the son to forgive him. The son wept, embraced his father and kept repeating his new emotional discovery about his father, "Dad, you can feel, Dad, you can feel. . . ."

The mother joined the session and for the first time in over fourteen years of physical intimacy the family became *emotionally* intimate. They broke out of the robopathic role-playing of their family social machine and began to communicate in a humanistic way.

It is highly important for fathers and sons to have as clear and intense a loving-doubling relationship with each other as possible during Phase I, since these are the basic ego-forming years. The relationship between father and son during Phase I should be intimate and ego-blending because of the positive influence this will have on the son's personality formation. Another significant reason for the necessity of a close relationship during Phase I is that it will produce a positive foundation for the father's and son's turbulent and difficult interactions in their Phase II adolescent years.

PHASE II: THE ADOLESCENT YEARS: THE STRUGGLE FOR SEPARATION AND INDIVIDUATION

This period is a highly significant emotional time between father and son. The son begins to retreat from an ego-blending relationship between himself and his father. He wants the security of knowing his father is there for him, yet he has begun to strike out on his own and define his self in his terms. The normal son begins to strive to become an individual, and he distances himself from his father and relates more closely to his peers.

Many fathers, during this critical phase of their sons' individuation and separation, behave foolishly and exacerbate a naturally uncomfortable situation into a dreadful one. Where did the acquiescent little boy go? And who is this arrogant monster who, incidentally, is beginning to eclipse his father's physique and physical strength?

This phase of a father-son relationship is fraught with seemingly insurmountable problems. If the normal problems that emerge in this phase are not handled properly, the relationship can become a lifelong disaster for both father and son. Fuel can be thrown on the normal adolescent father-son fire and cause a major conflagration.

All this can result in incipient problems of stress that can later have a severe negative effect on a father's physical and mental health and his longevity. It is also during this phase that a normally rebellious adolescent can, if not handled properly, be propelled into a life of juvenile delinquency or mental illness through improper treatment and unnecessary conflicts with his father. All of these more serious problems can be avoided if a father and son have a good understanding of what is happening between them in this phase of their relationship.

The Phase II socialization period is characterized by the son's developing sense of his own identity, not only in relation to his father, but toward the world in general. He may begin to act in a rebellious manner. He normally becomes belligerent about his ideas and opinions, even when he knows he's wrong. He wants to do everything his way. He is apt to become naturally rebellious, if only to feel his own ego power and to begin separating from his father and his family and becoming a person in his own right. If these normal expressions of rebellion which reflect his search for identity are squelched by a repressive father, his emergence as a full, spontaneous, creative man can be retarded.

One of the son's major adversaries, or "natural enemies," in this phase is his father. A father and son become engaged in a normal psychodrama where the son is the main protagonist and the father's role is enlarged. In psychodrama terms the father becomes the son's experimental *auxiliary ego*. The auxiliary ego in the form of the father represents all others in his life onto whom the son projects negative and positive emotions. With a compassionate, loving father the son can try out a variety of outrageous attitudes and behaviors without being hurt by his loving auxiliary-ego father, who absorbs some but not all of his son's punches.

The common sport between father and son of playful physical aggression in a boxing or wrestling match has all the ingredients of their larger loving conflict that centers around social and emotional issues. In a physical encounter, the father is usually bigger, stronger physically, and a more experienced fighter, and in nonphysical ones, also more experienced. A loving, understanding father lets his son throw a lot of practice punches to test his strength and ability, both physically and intellectually, without returning a knockout punch.

In contrast to the compassionate father, psychopathic macho fathers may hit their sons with knockout punches because they are stupidly blind to the realities of the jousting. They are unaware that their sons are testing their social and emotional strength, and that they need a safe person—the father—as an auxiliary ego. A son who feels safe with his father can role-test his new views and perceptions of the world on him. His father will absorb some of the blows.

In the son's real world of teachers, peers and school, if he acts experimentally there may be harsh reactions of condemnation or ridicule. But with a loving father as the auxiliary ego, the young man can test out and experiment with his behavior and attitudes, and an understanding auxiliary-ego father will provide valuable suggestions and nonpunitive feedback to his son.

Immature, macho or emotionally weak fathers will react as peers and outsiders, often in defense of their own weak egos. With this type of father the adolescent son will receive the same harsh punitive response he usually gets in the larger community. The effects include inhibiting him, breaking his creative spirit and not providing him with the needed opportunity to role-test new behavior.

In contrast with this type of parent, a loving, compassionate father will permit his son to test out new emotions, ideas and behaviors without such negative consequences. A good father takes the time to provide this kind of experimental environment for his son. He gracefully becomes his son's auxiliary ego during the adolescent's difficult role-testing period between childhood and manhood.

Fathers should recognize that sons in this phase tend to have a normal role-confusion because they are at the same time children and incipient adults, socially, physically and emotionally. Their sons vacillate between being children and being adults. The father has to make an understanding adjustment to this phase of his son's life.

I cannot stress the "normality" of this conflict enough. The son is attempting aggressively (sometimes violently) to clearly define his own ego boundaries and power without his father's influence. His father must understand this and provide positive, generally nonpunitive feedback.

The father who doesn't understand his son's ego needs at this stage can perpetrate a rupture in the relationship that is apt to be detrimental to both father and son—especially the son—perhaps for life. A son's casual drug use, delinquent patterns, neurotic perceptions of life—common and almost typical behavior of adolescents—can be hardened into more sharply defined drug addiction, delinquency and mental illness by fathers who do not understand this phase and fail to roll with the punches they inevitably receive from their struggling sons' experiments. The model is one of riding a bucking bronco. A father must flow with his son's efforts to throw Dad off his back, and yet hang in there sufficiently to maintain contact and be available for much needed information, guidance, and loving, appropriate, control and discipline.

Discipline Extreme disciplinary reactions by a father during Phase II are usually damaging. Heavy punishment and control can break the spirit of the adolescent son and damage his developing positive ego strength.

The disciplinary process becomes one of the paramount areas of father-son interaction during this phase. An important dimension of this process is that a son often compares his father's disciplinary response to his behavior with his friends' fathers' approaches. Two fathers may respond entirely differently to the same behavior, based on their own social contexts and values.

An interesting case in point is related to a son's smoking marijuana, and the different types of disciplinary response by two fathers from whom I acquired in-depth interviews. At one extreme was a macho father, an alcoholic who battered his son unmercifully because his son smoked pot. In fact, he kept his son locked up in his room "under house arrest" for several weeks. During this period he beat the son sporadically. The man used the situation and his son as an outlet for the enormous hostility and rage he had toward life in general and probably toward himself and his personal drinking problem. Needless to say, the father's extreme discipline had little positive effect on the son in dissuading him from marijuana use. In fact, the boy, partly to assuage his increased pain and violent feelings toward his father, graduated to the use of the arch-tranquilizer—heroin. This father and son became enemies from then on.

At the other extreme, a buddy-type father whom I interviewed smoked dope regularly with his fifteen-year-old son. His indulgence of his son, who was totally undisciplined, took a bizarre direction which manifested itself at a party at their home. After dinner, the father, a successful businessman, came out of his study enraged. He called his son down from his room and raved at him. "You rotten bastard. Don't I give you enough money for dope? I know you've been into my stash—there's a whole lid of grass missing from my desk!"

The son shrugged his shoulders and went back to his room. Everyone within earshot of this abysmal father-son situation was embarrassed and tried to act as if it hadn't happened.

Fathers in this phase are very responsible for helping a son develop a superego (conscience) that will enable him to become a more civilized person and an effective adult. Extreme punishment or extreme permissiveness are both ineffectual toward this end.

The discipline process in its broadest parameters determines the socialization of the son and his self. Each disciplinary act between a father and son is of enormous significance to both of them, especially the son. This is true for every act from a raised eyebrow to the extreme of throwing a son out of his father's house.

A crisis situation produces a deep interaction between a father and son, and invariably calls for a close examination or analysis of the problem and their relationship, and some subsequent disciplinary action. The father's method of discipline can be destructive or positive. When it is destructive it involves *personal* attack, no lesson is learned and both father and son feel they've been wronged by the other.

In the process of my research I interviewed many well-meaning fathers who beat their sons to impose their values and influence their sons' behavior. In most cases excessive physical discipline doesn't produce positive behavior change and tends to affect the son's self-image negatively. The son who becomes a punching bag tends to develop a low self-concept, one that will haunt him throughout his life.

There are two basic elements operative in any disciplinary effort toward behavior change, control or personality development between a father and son. One is the son's *ego or self-concept*; and the second is his *behavior*. A father can and should make clear to his son when he attempts to influence him that he always loves and respects him as a *person*, even though at that point in time he deplores his *behavior*.

When he says, "You're a rotten kid," is he referring to the boy's self as rotten or is he referring to his behavior as rotten? The point is that ideally a father should only characterize the behavior as negative and maintain a high regard for his son as a person. The behavior should be condemned but not the person.

I once intensively studied a father who beat his teenage son frequently, most of the time for no reason other than the father's own problems. The impact on the son's perception of the world and his personality was horrendous. The young man had a sense of total worthlessness. His value to his father was that of a punching bag—an object of negativity and hostility. This boy's negative self-image created by his father in his teenage years is likely to be a lifetime plague for both of them.

In contrast, in another case I interviewed a father who deplored his teenage son's negative behavior, mainly because he basically saw his son as a wonderful person who could surmount any obstacle. He would point out, "*You are great* but you are *behaving* badly." This young man developed a very positive self-concept that will probably serve his self-interest throughout his life.

The father who brutalized his son struck the young man's sense of self-worth and negatively affected his behavior. The positive father never damaged the tissue of his son's ego. He maintained a sacrosanct positive attitude toward the son as a person. When he was critical of or disciplined his son, he dwelt on the theme of how a fine young man like this was acting out in a negative way to his own detriment.

Bear in mind that discipline isn't always a straight act of disapproval, or a spanking. It can and often does significantly involve the withholding of love, and in effect this is a form of rejection. A forty-five-year-old physician I interviewed told me with great anguish about his father's constant belittling of him. "Since I was a little kid he picked on everything I did. Nothing I did was considered okay by him. God, how I hungered for that man's approval. From my therapy I've concluded that one of two things operated. One, he didn't know how to give approval. Or two, he somehow believed that that's what a father is supposed to do. Anyway, even though he died over ten years ago, my father's disapproving tape is in my head—and whatever I do seems to be in search of people's approval. I'm really a prick underneath, but I always play Mr. Nice Guy because I desperately want everyone's approval. I probably became a doctor partly because patients give a lot of positive strokes of approval. I'm sure all of this has to do with my father's inability to give me the approval I wanted and needed." This doctor's needs are felt by many sons who had fathers like his, men who held back their love and approval as a disciplinary device.

Sometimes the absence of discipline becomes a problem between father and son. One sixteen-year-old gang member I interviewed who was in prison for murder told me about the following incident between him and his father. "I'm really pissed off at my father. He should have got on my case. Like a week before we killed this guy, he found a 'home-made' [gun] in my room. I knew he saw it, but he never said anything. All he did was tell me I was just like my older brother who's in the joint [prison]. He'd keep telling me that. So finally I felt, fuck it, if that's what he thinks, I'll be like him. I didn't care anymore. I don't care that I killed that guy with that gun. My old man should have taken it away from me."

The doctor and the killer are both projecting the blame onto their fathers. Other variables obviously enter into their respective personalities. In a very significant sense, however, there is validity in their after-the-fact analyses that their fathers by their disciplinary stances were instrumental in affecting their negative behavior.

A father's style is a determinant of the disciplinary process he uses. In roughly 80 percent of my research sample, the central disciplinary approach was determined by a father's style. Macho fathers were most likely to employ some form of tough "manly" corporal punishment. Macho fathers who used physical punishment (within reason) were reasonably effective in socializing their sons, when they tempered the punishment with consistency (no hysterical outbursts). They were fair enough to state clearly the reasons for their discipline. A psychiatrist friend of mine, who lived on an army base for a number of years and did an on-the-scene study, confirmed that macho army men who disciplined their sons in this way were very effective in socializing their sons.

Fathers who have either psychopathic personalities or are egocentric fathers (as a result of their occupations or life situations) are the worst fathers with regard to discipline and its consequences. Their sons do not develop a rational sense of right and wrong from their fathers because this type of father usually punishes indiscriminately. Because of their irrational, emotional disciplinary approach, they produce rebellion and hostility in their sons and they teach them very little. The sons become geared to responding to their fathers' emotional outbursts, and they do not develop internal controls of their own. This type of discipline damages a son's sense of self-esteem, and tends to negatively affect his behavior.

Overly indulgent fathers tend to smother their sons with approval and are usually nonpunitive. They tend to give their sons overinflated egos and feelings of self-importance, which may not produce too many problems in the immediate family situation but may negatively affect the sons' life chances when they go out into the world. There, their exaggerated view of themselves, created by their families, may produce problems when they come into contact with people who care less about them. When confronted with the cold standards of life and reality, they may feel a sense of injustice. They may respond by acting out in a self-destructive, rebellious manner.

An overindulgent father can have a negative impact on his son by smothering him and inhibiting his natural tendency to become a person in his own right. He can drown his son's self-hood through various responses to his misbehavior which do not foster rational learning and personality development. This type of father sometimes attempts to control his son by instilling a sense of guilt into his psyche. How can the son get angry at someone who is so good to him and gives him everything? When this type of father punishes his son by putting on his hurt look of disapproval, the son is bound to feel guilty.

Overindulgent fathers can perpetuate their sons' problems through a *rescuing* syndrome. This type of father has not moved out of the ego-blending phase of his son's adolescent period. In such cases the father is so overidentified that he doubles with his son to the point where the son's misbehavior or problem becomes the father's problem. In the rescuing process, the father does not permit his son to confront the consequences of his actions. And what the father does, in effect, in this syndrome is prevent his son from facing the real world and the consequences of his behavior. The father, by overindulging his son, despite the fact that he does so out of love, is moderating the real world for his son. Because of this, the boy is prevented from developing his own ego ability to confront the adversities of life. This symbiotic relationship which is appropriate during most of Phase I is self-destructive for both father and son in Phase II.

In one pronounced case of this type, an obviously overindulgent father came for help to a therapy group I ran. His teenage son obviously dominated the father, and was always in trouble in school. It became apparent in several sessions that the son had a sense of injustice about the way his teachers treated him. In reality, his teachers would not permit the arrogant young man to treat them the way he treated his father. The son felt their demands for normal civility and respect were unjust, and he reacted with hostility. In therapy, the father and son began to better understand the dynamics of the situation, and the son's behavior improved. As he began to treat his father with more respect, he began to behave in this more positive way with other adults, including his teachers.

Permissive fathers who totally accept their sons' rebellion, deviance and neurotic behavior during Phase II are performing a disservice to their sons. In their sons' eyes they have caved in to accepting behavioral patterns which the sons themselves don't wholly approve of. A teenage son tends to have contempt for his father's total acceptance of ideas or behavior which he himself may question. As one fifteen-year-old told me about his permissive father: "He's really a ball-less wonder. My mom controls him and anything I do is okay too. Sometimes I wish he would take charge, because I have to admit I don't always know what's right."

Physical Power A normal problem between some fathers and sons in Phase II involves the change in physical power. Though the disparity in chronological age remains constant throughout life between father and son, the precise physiological differences between fathers and sons vary radically from one period to the next. The disparity between a father and his infant son is, for example, far greater than that between a father and his adolescent son. The contrast between an adolescent and his father is that between a person who is reaching his full physical powers and one who is losing them. A father between forty and fifty who has a late-teenage son is in a physically inferior position.

The effects of physical change on the father-son relationship parallel the effects of change in attractiveness on the mother-daughter relationship. Many self-centered mothers who have felt powerful because of their attractiveness become jealous of their developing teenage daughters' beauty, and this sometimes leads to unconscious conflict.

As fathers become physically weaker with age, their sons move into their years of peak physical strength. The physical conflict and play between a father whose physical power is waning and a son who is reaching the zenith of his physical ability can be loving and playful, but sometimes become serious. My own son, who loves me, thoroughly enjoys lovingly wrestling me to the ground. As he does so, he usually ignores my playful and sometimes serious protests. He enjoys demonstrating to me the changed balance of physical power between us.

This changing physical relationship between macho fathers and their sons tends to produce enormous conflict and negative competition. The proper response is for both father and son to acknowledge this normal shift of physical power and to not make a serious issue of it.

Macho fathers who resist this normal change of physical power by making sure they win their battles with their sons can propel their sons into violent activity with their peers. When an adolescent doesn't win with his father, who tries to constantly prove he is stronger than his son, the son may displace his aggression elsewhere.

A conversation I once had with a bellicose problem youth revealed that his relationship to his macho father was crucial to his violent behavior. I asked him one afternoon in one of my daily discussion sessions with his group, "Why are you always getting into fights?" (He averaged four or five fights a week.)

"I always fight with my old man." (Laughter) "We really fight. Sometimes we knock things down off the table, roll around and all that. He beats me all the time, but I'm getting bigger."

Although he "lost" his fights at home with his macho father, who apparently needed to assert his physical prowess over his son, the son won most of his street fights. One week I kept a count of his fights and found a relationship between fights lost with his father and fights fought and won with his peers on the streets of New York.

In the course of my research, the majority of men told me about the significant day in their father-son relationships when the balance of physical power shifted. In one of the negative cases of handling this normal changeover, one son told his macho, physically abusive father, "If you ever lay another hand on me I'll beat the shit out of you!" In this case both father and son knew the statement was true, and it dramatically affected their interaction. This father never hit his son again, but some fathers utilize other areas of power to control their sons.

In more positive father-son relationships at this changing of the guard of physical power, the father acknowledges the shift with joy. One good father I know is a tennis fanatic, and brought his son up to be a good player too. He always won in the early years when they played each other, and then as the boy grew into his latter teens the gap closed, and eventually the boy was clearly better. The father was a very competitive player, but in this case he shared his son's pleasure in the role shift. Men who are secure in themselves enjoy watching their sons developing prowess in all areas of life, and such fathers do not become competitive with their growing sons or try to impede their development in any area of life.

Value Conflicts: Idealism and Reality In my earlier years of doing psychodrama one session stands out in my mind as it relates to value conflict between a father and son. I was invited to direct a session in an affluent home in a small town on Long Island. The group was mainly composed of wealthy Jewish married couples who had escaped from the pressures of Manhattan to their new lifestyle.

In the warm-up to the session, a nattily and expensively dressed man with a pencil-thin mustache stepped on stage to present his problem with his twelve-year-old son. The man was obviously in great emotional pain. As is customary, I asked him to present his problem before we role-played it.

"My mother and father were orthodox Jews. I grew up in the

Jewish ghetto on the Lower East Side. It took me all these years to get out of that deadly social environment. I have done okay in the world; I have a beautiful wife, my own business and a son who is a good boy. Let me correct that—he *was* a good boy. The last six months have been hell for me and him. We constantly argue and he has threatened to run away from home."

The group and I became increasingly curious about the conflict between this father and son. Finally the father blurted it out and began sobbing: "After all these years of self-improvement and hard work my son came home and asked to be bar mitzvahed! I told him there was no god—we're atheists—but he won't let up."

At first I thought the man was inventing the story, but his tears and emotional pain were real. We became involved in a two-hour session. In essence, what emerged was that he thought he had escaped from the religious and cultural roots he denied, but somehow his only son had picked up his earlier religious values. In a sense the son was using the Jewish religion as a weapon of rebellion, but there also was a large degree of sincere motivation on his son's part to become bar mitzvahed, even against his father's wishes and values.

Fathers and sons during the Phase II adolescent period not only have normal physical conflicts, they are apt to battle over generational value differences. In other times in more stable cultures and societies there were fewer value conflicts between fathers and sons. There were more precise definitions for relating. And in most cases there were clearer ways for males to move from adolescence into manhood. They did not have to fight their fathers for autonomy. It was granted if they conformed to precise customs and adhered to the rites of passage that were set down for moving from adolescence to manhood.

Because of the rapidly changing social situation in America, the expectations of a son are less precise and there is often a generational value conflict. It is increasingly difficult for a father to transmit precise rules of life to his son since the norms change so fast.

For example, in my adolescent years, probably less than one percent of adolescents ever smoked marijuana. Today well over half have tried it. My standards on drug use conflict sharply with those of the society my son lives in. My high school milieu was entirely different from his.

Other examples of vast generational change are found in mass-media entertainment, and the attitude about such matters as violence in the media. The movies I saw during my childhood years contained simple human stories and had very little violence. Today the movies are full of mutilations, grisly murders and outrageous horror scenarios.

My son is an aficionado of these modern horror films, and I detest them. He thinks they are fun and exciting, and I think they are crass examples of the product of the typical banal, narrow Hollywood minds. He sees them all, and I see only a few for purely sociological interest in understanding modern tastes.

In this context, my son recently had what would have been a horrendous emotional experience for me. The experience and his reaction to it reveal something about the conflict of perceptions in this generation gap. During the summer he became friends with a young man—I will call him Jim—a twenty-five-year-old who seemed more like sixteen, my son's age at the time. The "man" was quite immature and had the basic personality of the standard Hollywood hustler who was trying to break into the film and music business. He would do anything but *work* for his glorified and exorbitant goals. He did not have to work because he had a wealthy father who sent him a sizeable allowance. Mitch would tell me about his friend's escapades with dope and prostitutes.

Jim's story is rather complex, but the bottom line is that one day he got into an altercation (in my son's presence) with a man who lived near his apartment. Apparently Jim owed him money (probably for drugs) and refused to pay up. The man assaulted Jim. Jim went into his apartment, got a gun he had bought that day and shot his adversary in the head, killing him.

My son was an eyewitness to this horrible event. He was interrogated by the police for several hours. Knowing something about the impact of such bizarre emotional events, when I saw my son after the police interrogation, I pressed him to open up and freely discuss his deeper emotional feelings about his dreadful experience. He ran through it one time, and in response to my continuing concern about how it affected him personally, he finally said in an exasperated voice: "Dad, I know what you're getting at. But you have to understand. When you were a kid, if something like this happened to you, I know you would have been really upset. But it really doesn't bother me that much. I've seen plenty of killings on the tube and in the movies. It really is okay. You don't have to worry about me." Based on the emotional tone of his response, I accepted what he told me as valid.

My son, like others of his generation, grew up watching not only horror movies but television violence. There is research evidence to support the belief that this generation does not distinguish clearly between real violence, like war reports on the news, and fictional violence.

I am quite sure that there is also a generation gap in the perception of atrocities like the Holocaust. Fathers who were old enough to be aware of the awful realities of World War II no doubt perceive the grotesque pictures of the bodies piled high in the death camps much differently from their adolescent sons. For fathers who lived through that historical period, portraits of the Holocaust are horrendous. To adolescents, some of whom watch the totally idiotic TV series *Hogan's Heroes*—believe it or not, a comedy version of a Nazi prisoner-of-war camp—the Holocaust has limited reality. Such value conflicts, or differential perceptions and reactions to the same material, are significant vectors in the conflict between many fathers and sons.

Another arena of value difference between contemporary fathers and sons exists with regard to sexuality and male-female relationships. The data indicate that there are sharp value differences between a generation of fathers who saw women as sex objects and potential housewives and the current generation of male teenagers who see women as friends, equal partners in sex and potential work rivals in all occupational areas which were formerly the exclusive province of men. These differential values between fathers and sons naturally produce conflicts and negatively affect a father's ability to counsel his son in these areas.

Another aspect of value conflict between fathers and sons in today's complex society is that sons tend to be more optimistic and idealistic than their fathers. Most fathers have learned by life's hard experiences that the idealistic hopes they cherished when they were younger had to be discarded in the face of the harsh realities of life. Most middle-aged fathers regretfully compromise the poetic ideals and hopes for a new social order which they had when young. In their place they adhere to the pragmatic ideas current in society. Fathers are more likely than sons to confront the realities of life and to bend with them.

Young people also seem to have a sense of omnipotence, a feeling that nothing will harm them. When I ride with my son in his car I sense his optimism that the road will clear for him and that an accident is almost impossible. He is enormously impatient of older, more conservative drivers who from his viewpoint impede *his* progress. His arrogance in "giving the finger" to a tough-looking group of people in a car who get in his way makes me cringe. I have a realistic fear of retaliation from certain types of bellicose individuals, since I have experienced being threatened with a tire iron more than once in my life. We have totally different responses to the same situation. Mine is a realistic fear of a dangerous possibility, and his reaction is more likely to be arrogance, omnipotence and self-righteousness.

Fathers approaching middle age become increasingly resigned to the inconsistencies and injustices of life. The conflict between idealism and realism leads to a "normal" struggle between fathers and sons, and was never more rampant or virulent than in the late sixties. The conflicts that appeared throughout the nation, and especially on campuses, mirrored the battles between the "untrustworthy" people over thirty and their sons. Sons believed that any kind of social change was possible, and most fathers felt very little in the system could be significantly changed. The battle raged between teachers and students, fathers and sons, and the establishment and the young. The conflicts which resulted from the effort to "green America" and stop the war have been partially resolved. However, the clash between conservative reality and radical idealism was dramatic and profound. It mirrored on the societal level the clash on this theme that goes on in the home between fathers and their adolescent sons.

During this so-called "hippie period," many sons abandoned their fathers' worlds, often leaving them with a sense of confusion and depression about the meaning of their lives. A son's drop-out behavior was construed by most fathers as a direct attack on the type of life they had built and offered their sons. As a result of the value conflicts during that era between fathers and sons, many sons left home for greener pastures. There were many hippie "gurus" who served as surrogate-father replacements for their own "uptight," "square" fathers in the peer communes that existed in those days. In these communes many adolescents found "selfless," democratic leaders with whom, if they were all properly stoned, they could share idealistic perceptions of the world and ideas on how to change it for the better.

The communes of the sixties have been replaced by the more fascistic mind-controlling cults of the seventies and eighties. Today many adolescents who have ideational or value struggles with their fathers seek nirvana in the numerous Jim-Jones-style quasi-religious cults that have proliferated in America. Cult-leader fathers like Jim Jones are magnets to "adolescent" people, young or old, who are disenchanted with their biological fathers and their seemingly narrow value systems. Such cult fathers appear to offer the possibility of nirvana, which is absent from the more honest and unsure fathers' repertoires of offerings. They also hold forth the idealistic promise that their movement will "save the world." This extravagant idealism that has in reality a limited chance for success is quite attractive to many adolescent minds.

Unlike the "hang loose," "do your own thing" guru fathers of the sixties, today's cult fathers of this type tend to see control and discipline in clear-cut terms. Total obedience is demanded by such surrogate fathers, and adolescent people voluntarily place themselves in this type of cult-leader surrogate father's straitjacket.

Contemporary cult fathers are often cold-blooded dictators in religious-leader disguise. They mask their macho extremist disciplinary approach to their "children" in a psychotic combination of fake sociopsychological jargon. A cult father I interviewed presented his approach to social control in his self-defined "religious" organization as involving "a total capitulation to our rules and regulations. These are precepts which flow from God. And if our children don't obey God's will they must be punished." Life in the cult situation tends to become a conditioned-response maze where the surrogate-father cult leader and his disciples control their followers' lives. In these contexts, as with the psychopathic macho father, the son does not adequately develop his own inner controls. The development of these inner controls is necessary for the adolescent to develop his own autonomy and become a mature adult. Surrogate-father cult leaders, like psychopathic macho fathers, do not want their "children" to become adults because they will then totally lose control over them.

The price the adolescent (of whatever age) pays in the autocracy of the cult is the relinquishing of his ego to the cause. The cult father expects, demands and receives total capitulation to his "idealistic" view of the world. No independent ideas are acceptable. The lure of cult fathers and their simple and clear rules is that the individual doesn't have to struggle and think for himself anymore. He gives up the attempt to communicate with his own father and the complex world he confronts, and moves into a situation where all of his needs are seemingly taken care of in an all-encompassing way. He has no struggle with the cult father. He has only one choice, and that is total obedience to the rules, dictates and controls of the "father."

Clever cult fathers are not blatant dictators. They deviously give the adolescent a sense of being independent and free when in fact he is a prisoner. The "delusion of independence" is characteristic of cults, but the reality is that any conflict with the cult father (or as with the psychopathic macho father) is seen as an act of rebellion that must be quelled. No deviation from this type of extremist father's norm is tolerated. The adolescent who "escapes" from his psychopathic macho father and joins a cult invariably finds himself brain-washed and entrapped in the delusional system of the benevolent-despot cult father. He has jumped from the proverbial frying pan into the fire.

In summary, it is apparent that many thorny issues and normal problems exist during the Phase II adolescent years between father and son. In these turbulent years there are many traps and tragedies that can result for both if they are not aware of various pitfalls, and if they fail to handle their problems correctly. In order for a father and son to go through their adolescent-relationship phase effectively, the following developments should take place.

In Phase I there should be a healthy ego-blending doubling relationship between the father and his son. After this, in Phase II, beginning at around thirteen the son should start to break away from his father, and a normal rebellion should ensue. Good fathers begin to let go with some reluctance, but should be on call to continue to guide their sons along positive lines. A reasonable father should give his son *his* school, *his* team, *his* choice of friends.

Bad fathering involves holding on and struggling to perpetuate the almost complete control once maintained over a son when he was a child. This produces head-on collisions and fights, resulting in the breaking and subservience of a son who might be reduced to a lifelong son-type position with his father. Some sons, out of revenge, break away from a father who does not let go and fall into rebellious, delinquent activity. In extreme cases, some sons break away from their "bad fathers" and turn to dictatorial cult fathers.

In my own case, letting go of my son at the right time during his adolescent years was a traumatic yet valuable experience for both of us. Up to his second year in junior high school, I was overly involved with him in terms of his physical and emotional health, who his friends were and his various activities, especially school. My involvement was a demanding, stressful responsibility that I felt was necessary.

When he was around fourteen our relationship became very difficult and full of traumatic incidents. In my zeal to control him properly and direct his life, I would resort on rare occasions to corporal punishment, namely a swat on the behind. This was met with a threat by him when he was fourteen to hit me back if I, *ever* hit him again. He never carried out the threat, partly because I backed off and partly because of his positive feelings for me.

On those rare occasions when I struck him, I was immediately filled with remorse, because I had done something I personally detested and disapproved of. I only did it when he defied me and

I lost control of myself, but during the fourteen-year-old period, there were several such head-to-head encounters.

A professional colleague with whom I discussed my problems was enormously helpful to me at this point. Basically he told me to let go of him. Even his school counselor told me one day, "Back off. Now is the time for him to sink or swim on his own." This was all sound advice. The time had clearly come (and passed) for me to cease doubling for my son and ego-blending with him.

The results of backing off were clearly positive. At fifteen he began to do better at school because it was now *his* school. He began to confront certain realities of potential career choices that he would have to handle on his own.

Moreover, there was an enormous personal gain for me. I stopped worrying about him and his progress on a daily basis. I felt I had raised my son—at least halfway down the line. I felt much freer to do my own work and deal with the conflicts and problems in my own personal and professional life. It was a liberating experience for me.

When a father backs off, the benefits for his personal life are not minor. The reduction of stress in a man's life is of enormous value; in some cases it may be a necessity. Fathers at this time should become therapeutically egocentric for their own benefit, and not only because it is of value to their sons' needs to individuate. In short, backing off at this time is a mutually beneficial act of fathering.

My relationship with my son improved enormously when I was no longer "on his back." He felt much freer about coming to me with problems he was experiencing. I became more of a resource than an oppressor. We became much more relaxed with each other. And my personal life was much healthier and happier.

Instead of my "coming on" toward him all of the time, he began to move more toward me. As I removed myself, I became even more desirable to him as a consultant in his life. In the past he would talk to me reluctantly—now he began to value my time and advice. We began to develop more of a man-to-man relationship which was blossoming into a two-way friendship. He was even helpful to *me* as a counselor once in a while. In brief, when my son reached seventeen, we were well on our way toward the highly desirable Phase III man-to-man friendship between a father and son.

PHASE III: MAN-TO-MAN FRIENDSHIP

The highly desirable result of the proper handling of the early years of ego-blending and the adolescent wars is that a father and son will in time love and respect each other as men and become close friends when the son reaches adulthood. In Phase III, a healthy father-son relationship uncontaminated by a Phase II holocaust of bad feelings, the son and father emerge as separate entities, *loving friends*, unscarred by their Phase II conflicts. They become equals who have a mutual respect for each other for the balance of their lives. They have mutual problem-solving experiences and thoroughly enjoy their productive friendship with each other.

This extremely rewarding relationship is not always achieved by fathers and sons. Too many father-son relationships become irreparably damaged and flounder in later years as a result of the ego wars of the fathers' and sons' earlier years, or remain stuck in some unresolved phase of the evolution of a father-son relationship. The man-to-man friendship between a father and son can be prevented by a number of factors in their earlier relationship. One is related to fathers who because of their own ego needs or cultural perspective do not let their sons become men. They have great difficulty in letting go of their "little boys." Some fathers behave this way because the "child" is the only one, in a difficult world which has them in an inferior subordinate position, over which they have control. In this situation a son may be mature in other areas of his life, but he remains subservient to his father when in his presence. In general, fathers who are insecure about themselves often attempt to keep their sons in the dependent-son role.

This type of father-son configuration was articulated in an intense psychodrama I directed with a young man about twenty-five years old. Frank had originally joined my group because of a problem he was having with his wife. We rapidly determined that the problem was at white heat when they returned from a visit to his controlling and domineering father, from whom he had not been emotionally weaned. Around his father, Frank acted like a little boy. His wife, who was in the group, noted that in his father's presence his voice even changed into something like a teenager's squeak. In his father's company he became a guilty little boy who had no opinion of his own and acquiesced to his father's view of the world. Their father-son relationship was not on a man-to-man basis because they were locked into Phase II. The father wouldn't let go and Frank did not know how to break loose from his hold.

According to Frank's wife, when they went home from a visit with his father, "sex was out of the question for days, because Frank acted like a petulant baby. He was depressed, guilty, and would often turn the anger he had toward himself onto me."

Frank's father would not let him out of his teenage phase even though he was now in his mid-twenties. It affected his marriage, and his role as a camp probation officer, where he became a son-type buddy rather than the more appropriate father figure to his wards. He would reinforce his wards' rebellious attitudes toward the authority figures at the camp. He obtained some psychological benefits from doubling with his delinquent wards against his bosses, the "fathers" who ran the camp. (In general, many revolutionaries and rebels carry on this type of struggle with their own fathers by rebelling against the larger social system. It is a form of displaced aggression against their real fathers from whom they are not free.)

Frank finally role-played standing up to his father after he learned the complex dynamics of his acquiescence to the hold his father had on him. The many role-playing sessions he had became a rehearsal for life with his father. He learned to stand up to his father and relate on a man-to-man basis in his sessions. As a result of his new ability his relationship with his wife and performance on his job improved significantly.

At first his father was very upset when Frank carried over his role-playing rehearsals into his real-life drama. Frank told the group how their relationship changed. "At first my dad freaked when I resisted his usual dictatorial orders on how I should run my life and even that of my family. I began to stand up to him much like I did in the sessions. I didn't knuckle under to him and I didn't rebel or disintegrate into anger. Those reactions from the past had always been ineffectual and self-destructive. I tried to reason with him and I was amazed at how much sense my arguments made. What also flipped me out was that he listened to me for a change, and did not treat me like a bad teenager. We learned how to talk on a man-to-man basis and we now have an excellent relationship."

The fathers and sons who transcend the Phase II wars and emerge as friends often work together in business and help each other with life's problems.

It is often remarkable and always gratifying to a father when a son helps him in his later years out of love and respect. One paradoxical man-to-man conclusion in this type of a father-son relationship occurred in the following case, reported in the press:

Tony Brooklier became his father's attorney in a trial for his life. Some might call him the Godfather's son. Tony Brooklier had to watch his father, 66-year-old Dominic, go on trial with four other men this week in an alleged Mafia case where the charges include everything from pornography, extortion and conspiracy, to murder.

There were temptations to liken the bond between Dominic and Tony Brooklier to the relationship between Don Vito Corleone and his son Michael in *The Godfather*, or that of Joe "Bananas" Bonnano and his son Bill in *Honor Thy Father*.

But Michael Corleone was just another hood and Bill Bonnano is an imprisoned screw-up. Neither turned out to be the man their fathers were. Tony Brooklier is different. He is not only Dominic's boy—in this alleged Los Angeles Mafia Boss Dominic Brooklier's toughest moment—he is also his father's lawyer. "How many fathers in Dominic's position," said someone close to the case, "would trust their sons to keep them out of jail? Legally, that is?"

When the trial began this week, Tony Brooklier had to sit in a packed courtroom as U.S. District Judge Terry J. Hatter, Jr. read aloud the lengthy list of charges against his father to the prospective jurors.

Tony Brooklier, who resembles Sylvester Stallone without

116

the smart-aleck smirk, looked away from the bench the entire time. His hands fidgeted with a fountain pen, and his stare focused on a four-inch stack of bound documents relating to the case.

Tony Brooklier appeared to be controlling a "cool," which in contrast, seemed second nature to his father.

During the reading of the indictment, Dominic Brooklier, a handsome, distinguished-looking man with hair so gray it looks minted, leaned forward from his green leather chair and listened intently.

The expression on his face never changed. Why should it? Few people know his 34-year-old son the way he does. Anthony is the oldest of Dominic Brooklier's three sons, and he hadn't raised a son, put him through college at Loyola and law school at UCLA, to come this far with him and then have doubts about his own flesh and blood. . . .

Tony Brooklier is, as his father's friends know, Dominic's boy. . . .

"Tony," said one of them, "is the son every father dreams of having but few fathers ever wind up getting."[3]

Like the Brookliers, most fathers and sons, if they arrive successfully at their man-to-man Phase III, become friends who help each other through the trials of life. In some cases, however, especially when the father is a competitive person (for whatever psychodynamic or social reasons), the father and son become competitive with each other in a different Phase III man-to-man relationship.

The competitive scene sometimes develops because the father perceives his son as an adversary for his power. In other cases the son, who now has matured and has some skills in life, may decide to get even with his father for certain Phase II offenses he believes were committed against him as a teenager.

The competition may be a mutual activity that becomes paradoxical when the son fulfills his father's hope that he become a competitor. In this regard I recall one father, a successful businessman, telling me in a session with great enthusiasm and a tinge of envy about his twenty-five-year-old son. "You know, the little s.o.b. has already made his first million. At this rate he'll easily become richer than I am."

Many sons avoid inevitable competition or comparisons with their fathers in convoluted ways. A psychologist, who is a leader in the field of group psychotherapy, told me, "My boy is a good therapist. But he told me the other day he never does group psychotherapy in his practice. He avoids being compared to me like the plague. He knows he'll never be as good as I am!"

An interesting case of a father and son, Darryl and Richard Zanuck, illustrates how love and friendship can characterize the man-to-man phase of a relationship. Regrettably, largely due to the competitive nature of Darryl, the father, in their later years they became locked in a dramatic struggle over control of a film empire. It was an affair that received worldwide publicity.

Darryl and Richard Zanuck were both internationally famous film-makers in their own right. The background of their struggle reveals the nature of the different phases of the father-son relationship. Their relationship was mostly positive during Phases I and certainly so in Phase II. However, it deteriorated for a time in Phase III largely because of the father's enormous competitive ego needs.

Darryl F. Zanuck was a pioneer in the film industry and founded the 20th Century Fox studio in the early halcyon years of Hollywood. He made hundreds of classic films including *Snake Pit, Grapes of Wrath, The Longest Day, All About Eve,* and *The Sun Also Rises.* During their father-son battles of the early seventies over the Fox studio, that last title was irresistible to many reporters for the purpose of facetiously characterizing their father-son relationship. Mel Gussow, Darryl Zanuck's biographer, used a book title that was both one of Zanuck's favorite phrases and a description of his personality: *Don't Say Yes Until I Finish Talking* (Doubleday, 1971).

His son Richard succeeded without benefit of nepotism. Through his talent and the early constructive nurturing of his career by his father, he rose in the hierarchy to become president of Fox when his father was chairman of the board. Richard, unlike the sons of many celebrity fathers and largely because of Darryl's fathering skills, emerged as a successful person in his own right.

The dynamics of their father-son relationship and normal struggles parallel the life-phase evolution of many fathers and sons whose lives were not in such a public spotlight. Their relationship, interactions and conflicts were articulately presented to me in several lengthy interviews I had with Richard Zanuck.

"When I was a kid my dominant reaction to my father was fear. He was a very competitive and flamboyant man who had a short temper when anyone got in his way or disagreed with him. That didn't mean that he wasn't capable of tremendous love, but he still had an explosive short fuse if he didn't get his way.

"I think what I suffered from as a kid was the same thing others suffered from who had to go to his offices and work with him. I don't think I was unnecessarily picked on, any more so than his associates. His temper was part of his great enthusiasm. When he was positive he could make you feel great. But there was always this feeling that he was a walking time bomb. It was a thin-ice situation and he was liable to explode at any time, especially if he felt you had crossed him or disagreed with him.

"Because of his personality, his success and his enormous ego, he was a distant figure as a father during my childhood years. [Phase I] It was hard for me to go to him and have a father-son conversation on the most basic levels. This was partly because his working habits were so strange. Weeks would go by where I'd never see him, even though we lived in the same house. I would go to school in the mornings and come back and he would still be sleeping because he had been out late the night before. When I left for school in the morning he wouldn't see me and he wouldn't come back from the studio until two or three o'clock in the morning, every morning. On the weekends he'd leave on Friday right from the studio and go down to the house in Palm Springs. So literally weeks would go by and I wouldn't see him when I was a kid. [Clearly Darryl was a distant father during Phase I. He did not exhibit any of the behavior patterns associated with loving-doubling fathers. In a way he was locked into treating his son on more of a man-to-man basis, the same manner in which he related to his work associates.]

"Although he was gone a lot his presence was felt. I always realized what a successful, powerful man my father was. But I didn't have the relationship with him when I was a child that I have with my two sons. With my kids every chance we get we'll be out in the yard throwing a ball around. We're very close. In my family we have a much more normal family setup than I had with my father. We eat together, I help them with their homework, we watch television together. To me, being a good father means doing a lot of things you don't want to do. Doing the dirty work, taking them to some kid's house, or having to take one of their friends home at night or pick somebody up—that's all part of giving time and energy to your sons and being a good father. I don't think that I love my kids any more than my dad loved me. But I'm growing up with them, in a closer way than my father did with me. I probably spend a little more energy and time than is really necessary. I think that I do it partly to compensate for the lack of those things that I felt in my relationship with my father. [Richard is apparently a loving-doubling father in Phase I with his own sons because he is painfully aware of what he wanted and didn't get from his father.]

"When I was a kid, before I became a teenager, he and I rarely went anywhere alone. I do remember a couple of hunting trips to Mexico when I was a kid. But there were always a couple of cronies of his around. As a matter of fact, I can't recall one instance where we went on any kind of an outing or ski trip or anything alone.

"I would have liked to have had that kind of relationship with him as a kid, although I'm not sure I would have liked to have gone off alone with him because of his attitude. He was a very scary person to me. I wasn't a shy little kid hovering in a corner or anything, but his presence was overwhelming. My father competed with and dominated everyone with whom he came into contact. This included big shots in the movie business, stars in his studio like Tyrone Power, Henry Fonda, Olivia de Haviland. Everyone feared him and capitulated to his domination, even tough adversaries like Jack Warner.

"One of my special memories as a kid, beginning when I was six or seven, was his showing films at home. We had a big screening room in our house and on Sunday nights a lot of movie people, stars and friends, would come to the screenings. I didn't really see these stars as special. A handsome leading man would come without his toupee and he would look ordinary. I'd overhear stories about their troubles with their wives or kids. They were my father's friends, and I never saw them as the superstars they were. I remember the star I was most impressed with when he showed up in person was Hopalong Cassidy. I was a fan of his movies. He impressed me.

"After dinner Dad would screen a film in our projection room. My two sisters and I seldom ate dinner with the grownups. We ate dinner alone, and then were allowed to come in and see the movie. My dad and I would usually sit alone in the back so he could be near the controls. He was bored a lot of times when he didn't like the movie, and he would begin to fool around with me. We would inevitably end up wrestling on the couch. Obviously, at that time when I was seven or eight he was a lot bigger and stronger than I was. But for him everyone, including his son, was a competitor. He would get me in a headlock, and then he would make me say the word 'give,' for 'I give up.' He loved to win, and he beat me regularly.

"We went through this ritual for a lot of years. When I was around thirteen there were a few times when I felt I might be able to get him. But he always managed to wriggle out of my headlock and get me. Then came this fateful night I'll never forget. I was now fourteen, and partly because of my dad's inspiration, I had become a pretty good athlete. He started his usual stuff of fooling around on the couch. I could just feel for the first time that I was stronger than he was. I got him in a perfect headlock, and I showed him no mercy. His face became all red, and his eyes were almost bulging. I just kept squeezing and asking him the question he had asked me all those years. He finally blurted out, 'give.'

"The balance of power had finally shifted after all those years of screwing around like that on the couch. It's an interesting highlight to me because it's so clear in my mind. I believe that was a turning point in my relationship with my father and the way he looked at me and the way I looked at him. Incidentally, from that point on, he never wanted to wrestle on the couch anymore. I mean, he didn't specifically say, 'Let's not do it anymore'; it just never happened again. He hated to lose at anything, even to his son.

"During my teenage years I started selling magazines on the Fox lot and I could often observe my father at work. The studio became like a second home to me, and my playground. I think hanging around there and naturally learning about movies got me interested in the business. My father never urged me to go into his business. It was almost a natural thing.

"This studio was like a little city within the huge Los Angeles metropolis, and it was also my father's empire. It's been like my home since childhood. I have no affection for any other place like I have for the studio, and I'm very comfortable there. This is an inheritance I received from my dad.

"My father generated a lot of enthusiasm around the studio and he would get me moving with that same energy. He had a personality that would make you get excited about something and make you work hard. He'd make you feel like you were the greatest thing going. You were writing the greatest script if you were a writer; or if you were a director, Dad made you feel that you had just directed the greatest movie. When I was a teenager he would give me the same kind of pep talk and slap-on-the-ass kinda thing that he gave his employees. So in spite of his distance there was his presence. I knew what was expected of me, in my behavior and attitudes. He set very high goals.

"I once recall him telling me when I was in high school, 'It just isn't good enough for you to be on the swimming team or on the football team. You've got to be captain and break some records.' He made you feel that you should and could excel. [Darryl transferred his occupational modus operandi from being a studio head to his relationship to his son. He was much like Bull Meechum in *The Great Santini*, a man whose father style flowed from his Marine Corps role. In fact, Darryl was a colonel in the United States Army during World War II.]

"He was very good at approval [reinforcement]. Because of his influence, in high school I did become captain of the football team and the swimming team, and president of the student body. I really can't tell you how much of my success was in my genes and how much of it was because he inspired me. He was like the head coach of the team that took care of me, which included my nurse and my mother. Although they took care of a lot of my needs, my father was clearly the inspirational force in my life.

"A lot of my father's messages to me during my teenage years were in the form of letters. I found out later he would tell his secretary to make some typos so it looked like he had done the typing himself and they were more personal. He would tell me he typed them because they were confidential—between me and him. His letters were like lectures. They were fascinating and instructional when I was a kid and even now when I reread them I find them of great value. Most of them were rather long letters, around five or six pages.

"Some of the letters would chastise me about getting a traffic ticket or a less than perfect school grade. He would write me letters about getting eight to ten hours sleep, about building up my physique and how important that was to a man. He would tell me to 'play it safe' with girls and make sure I didn't get any 'infections' from them. The letters made me feel good because he always balanced off the bad with the good. For example, he would remind me of my heritage. He would remind me that I had special advantages, and that I really had to live up to the family name. His letters made me feel, as he frequently told me, that I was blessed with leadership qualities, and because of that I had a special responsibility.

"He made me feel very special to him, compared to my sisters. I believe he did see me as someone in his own image. He always emphasized, even when he was disciplining me in the letters, that because I was his son I had special talents and could 'go all the way.'

[In the letters that I read, D.Z. seemed to be an excellent disciplinarian. He never attacked his son personally. He mainly chastised his *behavior*—and not his son's *self*. This probably was significant in Richard's development of great self-esteem. He interjected useful information into his messages to his son, information on how to live properly. It is important to note that D.Z.'s philosophical father message to his son was transmitted through his letters. Messages delivered by a father to his son in this form usually have a powerful affect.]

"What was my father's general message to me as a teenager? It wasn't just in the letters. When we were together, he made me feel special. He would kiss me on the cheek and hug me. There were several basic principles in his letters and talks with me. One was that regardless of my behavior, good or bad, I should always feel that I could tell him anything that I did. He never wanted to cut me off from talking to him about anything. He always used to say to me that the worst thing I could possibly do would be not to tell him when there was some kind of trouble. He felt that lying was a worse crime than actually doing something wrong. He wanted to maintain communication with me, and that was absolutely basic, whether it was about a sexual issue, or feelings, or things that I had done. He said, 'If you conceal something from me, I'm not on your team anymore,' which meant that I would lose him as the guy in my corner.

"I have reread his letters many times in recent years. The thing I get from his letters is that he was, in his way, a marvelous father to me during my teen years. He expected a certain level of performance. When my two young sons become teenagers I'm going to do the same thing with them. That doesn't mean that you have to go around cracking a whip all over the place, but what he did was instill a certain appreciation for my position and, thanks to *his* position, a certain recognition and an inheritance of privilege and power. He instilled in me the realization that I had many advantages, and that I had a certain responsibility to other people because of my position in the world. Basically he helped me to develop an ego strength that has served me well all my life.

"I've got to make one thing absolutely clear about my dad. No person that I've met in my life was more supportive than he was. I don't care if it was me or somebody else—when you had his backing he'd go all the way for you. I mean *all* the way. It was this quality that also made him so difficult to deal with, because if he went up against you, he would go all the way too.

"When you're dealing with a man who doesn't give a damn on any level, you're dealing with a very dangerous adversary. He'd go for broke whatever the issue was, even if somebody ended up getting killed. Of course, that's an exaggeration, but he would go completely all out. There was no holding back. If you were in an argument with D.Z. he wouldn't care if it resulted in his losing his job, or you losing your job. When he got into his competitive place, either you went down, or he would.

"He was terribly well organized in that respect, and he didn't waste his time or anybody else's time. He moved right in and said his piece. To his credit, he never held grudges. Once he got angry and told somebody off, the episode was finished. He wouldn't go around holding a grudge and saying, 'Oh, that son of a bitch did that to me,' for, you know, the next five years or something. It was finished. If need be, he would eliminate people from his life. He would consider certain people a waste of time and they would fall away from him by his design. It was this competitive ego trait of his that probably caused the big battle we had with each other at Fox.

"There wasn't any nepotism related to the fact that I became president of Fox around 1970. My father did help, but he believed I had earned the job. I began as a story editor fresh out of college. My father had no sentimentality about me in the business. He pushed me along because I was one of the hardest-working guys at the studio. I guess that extreme dedication to the business was inherited from him. When I became president of Fox, my father was chairman of the board. I was the number-two man at Fox. I should have realized at the time that eventually all D.Z.'s number-two guys got axed.

"In those days in 1970 he took me very seriously. He related to me on a man-to-man basis in a friendly way. He didn't treat me as a youngster, or even as his son. He believed in my judgment on a lot of things related to running the studio.

"I was running the studio, and he was in Europe fooling around. He had lots of women, and he became notorious at the gambling casinos all over Europe, and on the Riviera as an aging playboy.

"In some peculiar way during that period of our lives we had reversed roles. I became the father and he was the son. We had some very frank and strange discussions. They were quite unique in that I would be telling him as he told me years before, 'For God's sake, can't you go out with the same girl twice? Why do you have to have a different girl every night?' You know, that's just what you tell your high school son. 'You're staying out too late and not getting enough sleep.' 'Don't make a fool of yourself in public,' and those kinds of things. I became to him the voice of practicality and of realism. Sometimes he would abide by what I said because I was living a rational life at that time, and it made sense to him. I was a married man with my own children, and I worked hard at the studio.

"During that period, when he was in Europe fooling around,

I had many hard business decisions to make. He was acting foolishly and there were times when I had to cover for him. He was concerned with my efforts to try to hide his lack of activity. He became a little paranoid about my help, and he interpreted that as my putting him out to pasture. That's an exact quote: 'You're trying to put me out to pasture.'

"Actually, the reverse was true. I was trying to be loyal and helpful to him in maintaining his position. He misinterpreted my loyalty to him as an effort to unseat him from the corporation.

"Around that time we made several real financial bombs, like *Hello Dolly, Star!* and some others. The Burton-Taylor Cleopatra picture was an enormous financial catastrophe, and the studio was almost bankrupt. D.Z. felt he was losing his power and I guess he felt it was partly my fault. He came roaring back here to California. My feeling now is that he felt his power and his ego as a man were on the line.

"I'll never forget that fateful time, Christmas 1971. One day I was president of Fox, the next day I was virtually kicked off the lot. And what was horrible about the whole scene was that my own father had engineered and executed my demise.

"After the board meeting that day when I was fired, all of the board members expressed real regrets to me. But I knew they were all in his pocket, and it was really his doing. I remember him sitting there, cold as ice, not giving an inch. They asked me if I wanted to say anything. I knew it didn't make any difference what I said. Finally I said, 'I would like to call my attorney.'

"After I called my attorney and came back, I remember him at the head of the table. He was sort of hovering around and he gave me a dirty look. He said, 'What took you so long? We've all been waiting here.' I said, 'If you don't mind, I had to call my attorney.' He was very cold-blooded about it all, totally detached. There was no father-son relationship at all. He was quite brutal. I had five years to go on my contract, but my employment was terminated.

"I went into my office to get my things together and a couple of the board members came in and said, 'We're sorry. You have a lot of talent.' But that was it. While I was packing, a humiliating thing happened that added insult to injury. My father had sent some security guards to my office to make sure I was leaving.

"When I left the studio that day I was really destroyed. It was like a death. I live at the beach in Santa Monica and for several months I spent day after day walking the beach, asking myself, 'What's this all about?' I had worked so hard. I was of course terribly stunned and shocked that my own father was capable of doing that to me.

"When I reconstructed what happened from his point of view, I decided he didn't feel he had wronged me, and he had no guilt about it. He simply felt he was losing control, and that for him was unthinkable. In business he couldn't care less who went down, even his own son.

"Thinking back, I'm aware that he had to be a tough guy. You didn't succeed or reach his level of success in this business, dealing with the kind of people he was dealing with, unless you were a very tough guy. You had to be domineering and ruthless. I do know something about Hollywood people. Those were the qualities that generally got you ahead in his day.

"You also had to have a certain amount of talent, perspective and dramatic understanding. But you couldn't even deal in the league he was dealing in without being tough and bursting with talent. He had those qualities and I always admired him for it, but I never thought his power would be turned on me the way it was.

"We didn't talk for quite some time after that trauma in my life. But then he became pretty sick in New York and he was hospitalized. When I heard about it I called him from L.A. and asked him if he wanted to see me. He said, 'Of course.'

"I felt it would be a good idea for him to return to the family home in Palm Springs with Mom. I checked with her and she agreed to the idea. He agreed with us and he went back there to spend his final few years.

"From then on he and I got along fine to the end. We never really discussed our clash. He saw nothing wrong with what he had done to me. To him, at the time it had been necessary. Of course I forgave him, because for most of my life he was a good father. I always loved him. God, yes, I always loved him. But it was a love mixed with fear and worship."

Darryl Zanuck was an autocratic, distant father who had many redeeming virtues. Despite his competitiveness, or maybe because of it, he gave his son a message to live by. This stemmed largely from the fact that during his son's adolescent years he reinforced his son's ego strength.

In terms of phase dissonance, his error as a father was one of almost always relating to his son on a man-to-man Phase III basis. Even when Richard was a child, D.Z. could not inhibit the driving competitive ego that emerged in his wrestling bouts with his young son. In Phase I, D.Z. certainly was not a loving-doubling father. His enormous preoccupation with the highly competitive world of Hollywood sharks at that time naturally spilled over into his relationship with his son and his family.

His continuing stance as a distant, authoritarian (but loving) father into Richard's Phase II adolescent years worked well. His discipline approach correctly attacked his son's bad behavior, but at the same time he reinforced the teenager's belief in himself as a "special person." This positive reinforcement was most important for Richard's self-concept, and gave him the power to succeed in the relatively ruthless Hollywood milieu. Another positive vector during the Phase II years was the father's image as a positive role model for the son to emulate. D.Z. showed his son the way without forcing his apparent cognitive map for his son on him. He no doubt wanted him in the movie business; however, his son followed in his father's path because he saw his father enjoying himself in his work and valuing his activity.

The Phase III years are a mixture of positive and negative factors. On the positive side father and son worked together for the most part in a productive association. However, the father's driving competitive ego inevitably came into play, even with his son. Interestingly, Richard's lack of anger toward his father for what he did to him at that point reveals that he understood his father's character, and to the end he felt very little hostility toward D.Z. In fact, the interview clearly revealed to me that this son understood his father's needs and even though he became a target along the way he bore no lingering resentments. In fact, he has fond memories about him, is grateful for the valuable "messages" his father gave him and loved his father.

One general lesson to be learned from the Zanuck father-son relationship and many others I have researched is that very few fathers are effective in all three phases of fathering. Some fathers are excellent in Phase I at being a loving-doubling father and are ineffectual in other phases. D.Z. was relatively absent during Phase I, but was excellent as the "field general" in Phase II by maintaining his distance, authority and availability for counseling. Also, we have to believe in the truth of Richard's continuing references to his father as an inspiration and heroic role model for him. In Phase III father and son had a good, friendly, man-to-man relationship—with one large lapse. When D.Z.'s competitive ego flared, the number-two man in his empire had to go, even if it was his own son.

Before a man becomes a father he should consider his relative strengths in each of the three fathering phases. Phase I fathering predominantly requires time and the ability to be a loving and compassionate person in the nurturing of a young child's developing personality. In Phase II, a father needs to be a knowledgeable, sensitive authority in dealing with a naturally rebellious half-child–half-man who is trying to separate from his father and define his own personality. A Phase III father requires the ability to relate to his grown son as an equal without domination. A father's awareness of the normal problems and the varied expectations of his changing role in the three phases can be of enormous value toward the goal of effective fathering.

CHAPTER FOUR

Family Dynamics: Mothers and Others

MANY PEOPLE AFFECT the interactions between father and son. The others who intervene in the relationship include, in varying degrees of involvement and impact, mother, brothers and sisters. Following divorce and remarriage, there are also stepspouses, who may either complement the relationship or cause problems between the biological father and his son. A son's peer group, friends, teachers and coaches also have their impact on the dyad. These others can have an enormous effect in positively or negatively filtering the interaction between the principals. They comprise the supporting cast of characters in the father-son life drama.

The others who filter the relationship between father and son are of importance when the two are living close together. However, when the father is distanced from his son by long separations, divorce or the demands of the father's occupation, the others become even more significant to their relationship. For example, a father away at war can be depicted by the mother as a remarkable heroic figure. Like Ulysses, his odyssey can be portrayed to his son in flamboyant style. Or, as is often the case, a son living with his mother after the parents have separated or divorced may have his father portrayed to him by his mother as a horrendous person to be avoided.

The son and the father who are distanced each have to create a mental image of the other. Distance involves the necessity of creating an image in one's mind without direct objective evidence. Psychologically, this process creates a larger-than-real-life internalization of the other. Because the relevant other is not physically present, there is room for extravagant imagination and distortions of reality.

Even when a father is dead his presence may be felt enormously, and may affect his son's life. A fifty-year-old man whose father died when he was eight described his continuing intense emotions about his father as follows:

"My father died of cancer at the age of forty-three, when I was eight. I remember he had a lot of warmth. He owned a fruit store and was well thought of. . . . I never really accepted the fact that my father died. I kept idealizing him, thinking he was working for the FBI or fighting Hitler, and that eventually he would come back. I reacted with tremendous denial. For years I imagined I saw people who looked like him.

"I have a very vivid memory of Sundays when my father would take us to the park, or sled riding. My mother always recalls these incidents in our lives and keeps him alive in my mind. My father was a strong, steady person with a great sense of humor and a twinkle in his eyes. I'm very much like him. At work I'm a prankster and like to fool around a lot. It's becoming more and more evident to me that I'm not separated from him. It's a little scary, because he's been dead forty-two years now, and as we're talking I feel as if he's right here with me now."

This man was not unusual in holding on to his images of his father. People who are important to us are held firmly in our mind's eye, and there is often a halo effect that develops with separation. This is especially the case if there is someone, like the man's mother, who keeps the memory alive.

Apart from images filtered by imagination and the descriptions of others, there is a "reflector" factor that is somewhat different from the filter. The reflector effect involves seeing the father or son in the company of others who convey negative or positive images. For example, if a son visits his father in prison or sees him constantly in the company of disreputable friends, he will receive a negative image. In contrast, seeing one's father as a celebrity receiving approval, awards and respect can enhance the father's image to his son.

This halo effect on a father can result from the approval of his son's peers. For example, I recall a new and approving light in my son's eyes about me after I had been invited by his teacher to lecture to his sixth-grade class on the subject of gangs. My halo effect in his eyes was enhanced by the fact that a tough "gang leader"-type kid in his class was so impressed with my talk that he respectfully asked me a number of questions about New York gangs I had studied and written about in my book *The Violent Gang*. After my lecture and the halo effect of his classmates' responses, my son gave me the most approval I had ever received from him in my role of writer. For the first time, he was interested in and wanted to read my book on gangs.

Fathers are also often impressed or depressed with their sons and develop images about their sons based on the reflector effect of their sons' peers. A journalist I interviewed, a man who didn't like his teenage son's friends and was concerned about his son's intellectual interests, related the following story: "I had very negative feelings about my son's two friends who practiced with him in their pickup rock band. They slurred their speech into a form of punk rock and dressed rather shabbily. I was relatively unimpressed but tolerant of the loud punk-rock noises that emanated from his drums, their guitars and their raspy vocals. I found out one day, however, that after summer vacation one of the guitarists had been accepted to and was off to the University of California, and the other one was headed for Princeton. My image of my son and my hopes for his educational future were elevated by the halo effect and reflection of his association with his two rock-band pals. If they liked him, as they apparently did, and spent much time in discussion with him, I had to conclude that his intellectual ability must be beyond what I thought, based on the dull conversations I usually had with him and his friends. There was apparently more there than met the eye."

The halo effect can take strange forms in the interaction between a father and son. I recall a poignant and depressing psychodrama I directed at a state hospital with a twenty-two-year-old man who was incarcerated for a number of attempted murders. The young man was acting out a significant scene in his life with his father. In the scene the young man presented himself to his father as an effeminate homosexual. However, his father, for personal emotional reasons, blocked and refused to acknowledge or perceive his son as a homosexual. It was only after Bill, the son, brought home a friend in full drag that the father acknowledged his son's homosexuality. It took the reflection of Bill's best friend as gay to get the message across to his father.

Most fathers develop their mental images of their sons through direct interaction. However, a son's teachers and report cards, coaches, ministers, employers and peers can and do significantly influence the father's perceptions. Fathers who are enormously "other-directed" or operate from a distance rely on the varied reports they get from others about their sons. The most potent filter and reflector in a father-son relationship is the woman who is both a mother and a wife.

MOTHERS AND WIVES

Of all the basic intervening people who filter and reflect the images, relationship and attitudes between father and son, the woman who is the wife-mother to father and son is usually the most significant figure of all. Mothers are constantly filtering and interpreting data about fathers to their sons. There is a world of difference to a son whether Mom reacts to Dad, who has had several martinis on his way home from the office, with a big kiss and affectionately joins him before dinner for a drink, or whether she begins to chastise and rail at someone she identifies as a "drunk-again alcoholic" when he enters the house.

An incident in my personal history serves as an interesting example of how a mother can be a significant interpreter of data about a father. The incident further reveals a great deal about the way my mother and father relate as husband and wife.

In the process of researching this book I naturally spent a considerable amount of time interviewing my own father, who now lives with my mother in Miami Beach. In one interview, I was talking to my dad on the phone and getting some information about our early years. Suddenly there was an interruption on the phone and my mother was on the line. "Mom," I said plaintively, "I'm interviewing Dad for the book."

Without missing a beat, in accordance with the basic lifelong relationship the three of us had, she told me, "Whatever it is you

133

want to know and he has to say to you, I know what it is and I can tell you better than he can. Just ask me."

By her comment she emphasized a basic truth about my relationship with and image of my father. My mother was always a significant filter and reflector of my image of my father, and the reflection was usually negative.

I vividly recall sitting at the dinner table with my two brothers and father and mother and cringing at my mother's attacks on my father. "Look at him," she would say in Yiddish, "his head and shoulders are bent down. He's a failure. He doesn't have the courage to get a better job or make more money. He's a beaten man." He would keep his eyes pointed toward his plate and never answer her. She never extolled his virtue of persistence or the fact that he worked so hard; instead she constantly focused on the negative and created an image to his three sons of a man without fight, crushed by a world over which he had no control.

His not fighting back against her constant criticism had the effect of confirming its validity to her sons. I have to add that my mother's treatment and depiction of my father did not convey to me that marriage was a happy state of being, or that women were very supportive people. I was not especially motivated to assume the role of husband and father myself from my observations of my whipped father.

In this same context a psychiatrist I interviewed told me of an incident in his own psychoanalysis during which he described his father to his analyst as basically a failure, without much heart and full of fear. His analyst pursued the description and they both concluded that what he was presenting was really the voice of his mother, and not his own opinion. When they bypassed and eliminated his mother as filter and reflector of what his father was like, the psychiatrist saw his father as a more positive and heroic figure.

My overall research clearly supports the fact that the mother is a basic filter and has enormous significance in the father-son relationship. One significant theme in the triad relationship among father, mother and son is the dynamics of the Oedipal complex. I do not perceive the Oedipal complex in strict Freudian terms, with its primordial, genetic or unconscious implications. I believe there is an overt "social Oedipal complex." By this I mean there is a triadic relationship between mother, father and son that has certain characteristics and natural conflicts that illuminate many social and psychological insights about the father-son relationship.

It is in order to first recapitulate the Freudian Oedipal viewpoint before analyzing its meaning on the contemporary social scene. According to Freud and his psychoanalytic concepts, a mother usually cares for her infant son in every vital respect, and she becomes a model to him for every love relationship. She kisses, fondles, pets him, may even playfully stimulate his genitals, all of which is pleasurable to the child. By her tenderness she awakens his sensual interest and prepares its future intensity. In brief, she teaches the child how he should love.

According to Freud, the child loves itself first and afterwards learns to love others, to "sacrifice" something of its ego for another. As a matter of fact, in the infancy phase there is no distinction between self and object. If the infant seems from the outset to love others, this is simply a manifestation of the infant's own feelings and needs. A boy's emotional development requires that he abandon, or rather subordinate, autoerotic satisfactions and substitute a "foreign" object for his own body. When this occurs he may, in Freudian terms, be properly said to love an object, or person, other than himself. Because the mother has been a significant person to him since birth, she becomes the first basic object of the boy's love. Freud further posits that the son naturally develops an "erotic attachment" to the mother. He often wants to and does sleep with her at night, is present while she is dressing and caresses her. With regard to erotic attachment to the mother, Freud postulates that the son's feelings tend to be unconscious and that he does not have a clear awareness of what is happening. The son has, according to Freud, unconscious sexual desires for his mother which he blocks through repression.

Freud assumes that the erotic attachment that evolves between a son and his mother is important to the son, and he jealously guards his mother against any rival for her affections. According to Freud, on the unconscious level, despite the fact that the son may love him, the father is the greatest and most formidable rival. The "little man" unconsciously would like to have the mother all to himself. The father's presence is disturbing. When the father shows tenderness toward the little boy's mother, the little boy is often irritated. He generally feels great satisfaction when the father is away at work or on a trip and he has his mother all to himself. In many cases the son gets to sleep in his father's place when he's away, and this generates further interest in the mother and unconscious hostility toward the father. From my viewpoint, all of this has validity in a social sense without any unconscious elements.

Frequently the boy expresses his loving and protective feelings toward his mother in a playful way and promises to marry her. As in the legend of Oedipus Rex, the son regards his mother as his, and this tends to produce subtle problems between father and son. This wedge in its extreme form causes the son to dream about having a sexual relationship with his mother, and in some cases to sabotage the parents' sex life.

A classic case of this sabotage emerged in a psychodrama session I ran with a young psychologist who was very upset about his son's behavior. He had a difficult "social Oedipal" problem —vaguely humorous—that revolved around him, his wife and his seven-year-old son. At the outset of the session the articulate father described the problem as follows:

"My sex life with my wife is a disaster because of my son. Around six months ago, he got into the habit of waking up at odd hours and coming into our room. His bedroom was next to ours in a small two-bedroom apartment. He seemed to have an unerring knack for arriving just when my wife and I were making love. He would either want a glass of water, to be with her or to tell her he was sick—all kinds of excuses. We had to respond to his needs. He always wanted Momma, and she always responded to his needs despite my later protests. Her response reinforced his behavior. She argued that his needs were real and I argued back that on some level he knew what he was doing.

"Anyway, the next logical step was to lock our door, since neither of us wanted to lock him up in his room. It didn't help because when he found the door locked he would bang it with his fists. No matter what we did, interrupted coitus and frustration resulted for me and my wife.

"One time my wife, in the throes of preorgasmic passion, agreed with me and refused to respond to his loud banging on the now locked door to our bedroom. He got a chair and almost knocked the door down.

"No amount of punishment or talking to him controlled his rotten behavior. He would say, 'I don't care. I was sick.'

"I might add I enjoy making love in the morning too—and he successfully killed that off as well.

"My wife and I were reduced to making love at odd inconvenient hours. I would run home from work when he was at school. A few times we got a babysitter and checked into a hotel."

In a follow-up session with the man I learned that the son finally grew out of this behavior when the family moved into a house where the son's bedroom was located much further away from their bedroom. In this session he commented on his past problem:

"My analysis of it? It was Oedipal. He wanted Momma and unconsciously he was aware of his interference with our love life. When I think back, our triangle was not only sexual in nature. My son and I were in conflict for my wife's affection in other aspects of our life together."

What usually happens to the triangle is that the son, on entering adolescence, lessens his emotional demands on his mother and his subtle, unconscious, hostile feelings toward his father. A corollary result is that he starts to become closer and more accepting of his father.

According to Freudian theory, however, the importance of the Oedipus complex has by no means vanished by puberty. The son's sexual drives reach considerable strength and intensity in adolescent passion. The son normally frees himself from his parents and discovers another female whom he can love. Then the normal son tends to become reconciled with his father (at least with regard to this issue), since he gives up his mother as a sexual love object.

I do not subscribe totally to Freud's Oedipal theory. Some of what he states has meaning in understanding the mother as a filter, and the dynamics of the father-son-mother relationship. Unquestionably, the mother in most families is a nurturing love object to the son. Moreover, the son in Phase I of his relationship to his father tends to perceive him on many occasions as an interloper or someone who dilutes or takes away his mother. The son sees his mother as crucial to his life's development early on in many more ways than his father. His father's contributions to his life are usually less visible to him than his mother's more obvious activity. Because of this, and because of his love for his mother and tinge of jealousy of his father, a certain natural antipathy toward the father dilutes their relationship through early adolescence. When the son reaches the age of around fourteen, however, he can become closer to his father, since the son is now aware of other avenues of sexual expression with girlfriends. He can now usually detach himself sexually from his erotic feelings about his mother, and in a normal process among the three he begins to cease viewing his father as a rival for his mother's affection.

All these factors enter into the shift from Phase I into Phase II of the father-son relationship. The sharp edge of their competitiveness for mother diminishes; however, other normal conflicts between father and son emerge.

Notable in the emergence of problems is the fact that the father becomes more significant and pronounced as the transmitter of the rules and regulations of society to his son, and this begins to negatively affect the father-son relationship. Because his sexual jealousy for his mother was repressed, the son during his preadolescent years usually vents his hostility in this area openly toward his father. Now that the son is a teenager and normally in conflict with his father over the rules of society, the disciplinary process gives him an excuse to act out other feelings. His hostility may emanate more from his sexually repressed feelings toward his mother and his jealousy toward his father than from the discipline situation with his father; however, he now has a battlefield in the disciplinary process for conflicts with his father. Fathers, mothers and sons who are aware of and understand these natural dynamics may have a more harmonious relationship during this late Phase I to early Phase II period in their triadic relationship.

Another issue that arises during this delicate period is that mothers often become referees who temper Dad's rules. The mother often admonishes the father to go harder or easier on the boy. During this period, the mother is set up in a pivotal position of power, which is too often misused for her own emotional needs. More specifically, as pointed out, the son is trying to individuate and is locked into a natural conflict situation with his father. A mother can use the situation negatively for her own ends, for example, by allying herself with the son against the father and pointing him like a missile at the father to vent her own grievances as a wife against her husband. In this context I have observed that in family dynamics, some mothers use their sons as weapons against fathers to further their own interests in battles with their husbands.

Sometimes a social Oedipal triangle reaches pathological proportions and has disastrous results. The following case is an extreme one, but it reflects a sociometric triangle of conflict that unfortunately exists in many families on a less intense level.

A 16-year-old youth, trying to defend his mother from a severe beating, allegedly shot and killed his father yesterday in front of their home, police said. Acknowledging the mother had been beaten often by the father, police nonetheless booked the youth at Juvenile Hall on suspicion of murder. The emotionally distraught mother defended her son today, claiming the shooting was an accident that occurred while he was trying to protect her. "Any kid would try to defend his mother," she said. [She may very well have encouraged and approved her son's act.]

The mother, whose face was swollen and throat scratched from the beating, wept as she recalled the shooting and her past violent relationship with her husband. . . .

She said her son had fired the gun at her husband accidentally.

"He wanted to scare him because he had seen me beat up so often," she said.

Her husband had beaten her regularly for more than 10 years, she said, adding, "The police came by just about every week because of the fights."

In past fights, she said, her husband had broken her arm and leg. She said her son had witnessed much of the violence and "begged my husband not to beat me."

The couple had been married for 19 years. . . .[1]

When the hostility and violence reach these proportions the relationship will most likely end in divorce. Separation or divorce, however, does not terminate the process of manipulation in the father-mother-son triangle.

A recently divorced man told me how he had played a dishonest game with his ex-wife to further his relationship with his son. "I was very aware when I divorced my wife and she took custody of my five-year-old son that she had powerful leverage with me. Any positive feelings I had for my wife were dead, and my son was the only person on earth I really loved. She knew this. My wife took me to the cleaners financially and was a total bitch, and I agreed to anything she wanted. You want to know why I took a lot of crap from her and gave her more than she deserved? I wanted her to like me enough so that she would say nice things about me to my son. Maybe not nice things, but at least she wouldn't tell my son that I was a total rat. What he thought of me was very important to me, and I paid whatever price his mother asked in order to get her to give me a positive image with my son."

In another case that makes a similar point, a father went out of his way to minimize his alcoholic ex-wife's peccadillos and her negative image to his son. He was divorced from her and had custody of his son. The fifteen-year-old had enormous hostility toward his mother. The father worked hard at explaining the mother's problems and their causes to the son for the purpose of enhancing the son's image of his mother. He did not do this for his wife. He did this out of love for his son because he did not want the boy to be consumed with painful, hostile and negative feelings about his mother. He moderated her truly bad image for the benefit of his son. He told me he made his wife look good to his son because he did not want his son to "see women as bitches who try to castrate men. I wanted him to have a healthy attitude about women. After all, most women are not like his mother."

When a father is deceased, the mother plays a more crucial role in transmitting the father's image than when the father is merely absent from the home. In the case of one young man I interviewed, the mother had filtered and transmitted to the son an almost saintly image of his father which was a significant force in the son's life. The mother methodically created a positive image of the boy's father, who had been a physician. The mother's transmission was so powerful and positive that her son, then twenty, enrolled in medical school in an attempt to emulate his "sainted" father.

An interesting dimension of the situation was illustrated by the tearful and poignant comment he made during the interview. "I loved my father very much and still do. When I was little he had a red sixty-eight Cadillac. To this day when I see that model car, I speed up to see if it's my dad driving—even though I know it isn't and that he's dead. He's with me all of the time and very important to my life."

SIBLINGS

A question I have been asked almost every time I have taught a college course in juvenile delinquency over the past thirty years is "Why does one brother in a family became a criminal and the other one an honor student?" The question is usually followed up on with the naive statement: "After all, they both come from the same family."

The answer is that nobody is ever socialized by the same family as his siblings. As a case in point, my own family had one father and one mother, married for over fifty years, and three sons born about five years apart from one another. There were in effect four families. The *first* family that existed for two years was a husband and wife without children. The *second* family was comprised of a husband and wife and son, until that son reached the age of five. In that family my older brother Morris recalls having a young, strong father. "Dad was a powerful man in those days. I remember going up against him one day when I was a kid. I did something he told me not to do. All I remember was my terror of this giant man who gave me a good spanking. I was maybe three, but I don't think I ever misbehaved in Dad's presence again.

"I also remember Dad as a very independent guy in those days. Even though there were three strong women around, he had balls and did what he wanted to do. The three women were Mom; Dad's mother, who owned the six-family house and lived upstairs; and Mom's mother, Grandma Rachel, who moved in with Dad, Mom and me. In those early days he was the boss. I've never forgotten how when I was five he took me along with him to the Ford dealer in Irvington, New Jersey. He plunked down around 750 dollars in cash and we drove home in a brand new 1925 Ford flivver. He didn't consult Mom or anyone. He didn't have a lot of money from driving a truck but he saved it up and just did it on his own. I was really proud of him and respected him in those days. Later on, after that, I think those three women just wore him down."

When I was born in 1924, I entered an ongoing *third* family. I had an older brother who was a brilliant student with a high IQ. My brother, from my early years until I was almost twenty, seldom paid any attention to me. There was no sibling rivalry. We each did our own thing.

I had a progressively domineering mother, and a father who became more and more of a workaholic and weakling as the years progressed. In some convoluted way I became "the great hope" for my mother. She somehow manipulated me into promising her fur coats and other luxuries when I grew up. Those things, she told me, "a *schlemiel* like your father who works on a truck could never get me."

As our family entered the thirties after the start of the Great Depression of twenty-nine, we were poor and my father was sporadically out of work. I vividly recall him sitting in a little park near our 25-dollar-a-month railroad flat in a three-family house, totally dejected. He would often sit there with his head cupped in his hands, a defeated man and a weak father. I believe the women and the depression crushed him. During those early years, my mother became mother and father to her sons to compensate for the powerlessness of my father.

My brother Joe, born in 1928, was the youngest son in a *fourth* family. He entered a family which was different from the ones which Morris and I had been sons in. My father now worked six days a week on a laundry truck, left early, came home late for dinner and went to bed at an early hour. My older brother left home and married early in life. I became both an older brother and a kind of surrogate father to my younger brother Joe, in part to compensate for the fact that my father seldom functioned as a father to Joe. Older brothers often function as surrogate fathers to younger brothers when the biological father is either weak or absent.

In the four families I have described, each son in essence had a different father because of the changes in life circumstances. And in fact, one of the sons (me) became a quasi-husband to his mother and father figure to the youngest son. This change of father role in relation to the ordinal position of the sons is common to most family dynamics during the lifetime of the family. Euripides once said, "No man ever enters the same stream." To loosely paraphrase this concept, "No man or woman ever enters the same family."

The relationships of brothers is often affected consciously and unconsciously by a father. For example, competitiveness between brothers is often fostered or diminished by a father because of his own ego needs. As I have noted, many delinquents and violent gang members have successful and effective law-abiding brothers. The father, exhorting his pariah son to "look at how good your brother is," tends to deepen better behavior in the "good brother," who is really going to show his father that his confidence is not misplaced. The "bad brother" usually becomes further alienated, angrier and more delinquent as a form of rebellion against his father. He also feels he can never compete, at least in his father's eyes, with his sibling role model.

There are many cases in the Bible and other literature about the "good son" and the "prodigal son." Cain and Abel were one case. In John Steinbeck's book *East of Eden*, the "good son" and the "bad son" vie for their father's affection—and are both hurt in the process.

Loving noncompetitive fathers produce sons who are often extremely close. This is especially true of fathers who do not transmit excessively macho attitudes. A macho father style negatively affects warmth and compassion between brothers. It encourages macho characteristics of competitiveness, lack of openness, control of affectionate emotions and aversion to vulnerability and physical demonstrations of affection. As a role model, the father of the family sets the tone for the type of masculine style his sons will follow, and whether or not they will be competitive with each other.

Brothers are closer with each other and their family during crises. In many cases the only periods some brothers indicate as times of intimacy and sharing with each other occurred during crises in their family. During these periods an intimate bond between brothers is likely to appear. A family death, debilitating disease or a severe economic crisis often causes brothers to come together in a wonderful form of closeness.

Sisters often intervene in father-son relationships, and function in a positive way. Sisters, as reported in a research project by William Arkin, often fulfill needs not met by many fathers and brothers. On one aspect of his research, Arkin reports:

"The closeness between brothers and sisters manifested itself in the form of mutual aid. Brothers and sisters both reported that sisters more frequently than brothers assisted brothers with financial aid. Sister's piggybank was often raided to finance a date or the purchase of a needed item. Even in adult life, brothers sought out sisters for such financial aid and this was usually attributed to the fact that they were 'more understanding' or 'easier.' Brothers might also serve as family bankers provided the age difference was great enough to eliminate competitiveness."[2]

Arkin also found in his family study that sisters, more often than fathers or mothers, were helpful to their brothers when they needed advice on their male-female relationships. Men with sisters relate better to women in general. On this subject, Arkin found that sisters, not mothers, were the primary socializing agent for some men's intimate relationships with women. Men and women both indicated that men with sisters were more effective in intimate relations than men who only had brothers or were only children.

Sisters often function as sexual advisers for their brothers because parents—especially fathers—have difficulty discussing the subject with their sons. My own research revealed that fathers had difficulty communicating with their sons on their relationships with the opposite sex and their sexual activity. Because of this block between fathers and sons, the subject is often handled not by the mother but by a sister.

In reinforcement of Arkin's and my research, W. Toman found in *his* study that the oldest brother of sisters is apt to be a ladies' man who adores women not only as wives but also as friends, colleagues and lovers. The youngest brother of sisters also has success with women but in a different manner; he is adored by women who look after him. Sisters are seen as more active in role-shaping, since they are defined within a peer context regardless of age differences, while a mother is perceived as of a different generation.[3]

Sisters fill in for the fathers and mothers who have difficulty communicating with their male son on sexual matters. In brief, female siblings seem to contribute more than the mother to the son's ability to have successful relationships with a woman. Such cross-sex sibling socialization must represent more than just the experience of living together in a family environment. Contact with sisters seems to foster expressiveness and ease in relating, and thus helps men in their future relations with women.

My data reveal further that important aspects of a man's relationship with his spouse are determined by the way in which his father and mother related, for good or bad. Their relationship tends to stand as the basic role model for his own marriage. In my many years of psychodrama and group therapy, I have run numerous sessions where it was revealed that a son's relationship with his wife is a replica of the relationship his father had with his mother.

GRANDPARENTS

Grandparents, especially the grandfather, significantly influence the father-son relationship. When the grandfather is present, the son can sometimes witness aspects of the fathering process that occurred between his own father and his father's father. In addition, grandfathers can become on-the-scene coaches in the socializiation of their progeny.

A grandfather is at times a surrogate father. He can take over the father role with a grandson, especially when the real father and mother encourage him to do so. Part of the reason he can effectively assume the role is that at this late time in his life he often has the quality time and the inclination to father. He may have these attributes more in his later years than during his actual fathering years.

An interesting case in point of family dynamics that propelled a grandfather into a surrogate father role is delineated in the book *A Man in the Making*, by Dr. Richard Robertiello. His own father was, as he describes it, "busy glorifying himself as a doctor. . . . My grandfather became more of a father to me than my own father. Michelangelo apparently decided the day I was born and was a male that he would take me over, raise me, train me, and help me to become all the things he had always wanted to be. Everyone else in the house was too frightened of him and his temper to offer any opposition."[4]

His mother participated in the transfer of power because of her own personality. According to Dr. Robertiello, his mother "was a very passive, compliant, insecure woman who was dominated by her own mother and father. She was completely cowed by my father and grandfather. Her anxiety about her ability to cope was so great that despite the best of intentions she was not able to give very much affection to her son. She readily allowed the grandfather to assume the basic parenting role."[5]

Given this unusual configuration of a remote frightened mother and a success-oriented busy father, the son was in effect brought up by his grandfather, who became his surrogate father. Although his relationship to his grandfather was unique, it reveals the kind of role many grandfathers could play with their grandchildren if they chose to, or if they had to because of the absence of one or both parents.

"So there I was an infant, the first son of Attilio, handed over to Michelangelo for him to train to be what he, Michelangelo, was supposed to be but wasn't—the world's greatest genius and intellectual achiever. My grandfather was very Pavlovian in his methods. He used behavior modification—rewards and punishments. He worked with me constantly. When I was in second or third grade, I remember his sitting at the kitchen table with me for hours. We would go over my homework, spelling the words again and again until I knew them perfectly."[6]

Dr. Robertiello, in describing his relationship to his grandfather, comments on the problem of the lack of significant emotional communication between males, certainly between fathers and sons. His analysis has meaning for many men in American society, especially macho fathers.

I have never really communicated very well with my grand-father or my father or my male cousins or uncles or with my son or stepson. And they have never communicated very much with any male in their life—certainly not with one of their relatives. As a result, almost all of us men have been entirely dependent upon our women to provide us our feelings, or at least the outlet for our feelings. And we have been so afraid of losing that connection to our unconscious that we have been tempted by, and at times fallen prey to, the temptation of seducing our women, and controlling them so they cannot leave us.

In my family we attempt and sometimes succeed in killing ourselves. We literally cannot live without a connection to a woman. To Michelangelo and my father men were strong, hardworking, and practical; women were soft, romantic, and poetic. Women were the ones who could feel and care and love and be tender and considerate. For many men this ability has been so stifled by our society as well as by our specific family, that we feel lost and dead and gray without it and without women to provide it for us vicariously.[7]

Dr. Robertiello here describes a characteristic of many macho fathers who are limited in their ability to relate openly and emotionally to other men, including their sons. To overcome this deficiency a man should become a loving-doubling father to his son in Phase I of their relationship. Through this experience he helps to develop his ability to relate to both men and women emotionally and with compassion.

Fathers socialize their sons from the unique personality that is developed and passed on by the son's grandfather. The son inherits a variety of cultural and personality traits which are transmitted from past generations. These transmitted forces are built into the socialization process, and the generations of grand-fathers and their influence, which tends to be relatively invisible, remain a highly significant force in the socialization process of a young man.

In the case of grandfathers like Dr. Robertiello's, the impact is apparent. He was directly on the scene, and like the powerful (godfather) grandfather figure he apparently was, he more clearly affected his grandson Richard. In that case there was no special conflict noted between grandfather and son. In some cases when a powerful grandfather intrudes on a father's training of his son, the father becomes resistant. Despite these possible problems most grandfathers have quality time to spend with their grandsons and are accepted by their sons. They have lived their lives and usually have developed a level of wisdom and power that can be transmitted to their grandsons.

In the immediate situation, a grandfather can interact with his grandchild without any of the conflicts that can naturally exist between fathers and sons who may be going through a period of normal conflict, as in the adolescent Phase II period. A kindly grandfather can often play the role of a mediator and adviser who helps and solves some of the normal conflicts that emerge between fathers and sons, especially during the difficult teenage years. Grandparents can play an auxiliary ego back-up role as a father to their grandchildren, and can bring the cultural lineage of the family into the child's learning process.

Grandfathers can and should play an important role in sup-plementing the relationship between fathers and sons. Most fam-ilies have not properly accepted the valuable contributions that a grandfather can make to their interrelationships.

DIVORCE AND SEPARATION: DIVORCED FATHERS AND STEPSPOUSES

Divorce, which is steadily increasing, is more significant than death in distancing fathers from their sons. According to recent statistics, more than 50 percent of marriages end in divorce. This means that in contemporary society approximately half of all sons are distanced in some way from their fathers by the divorce situation. Also, since in over 90 percent of the cases of divorce a mother gets custody of the children, the problem of father-son separation is considerable. The nature of divorce can produce alienation between fathers and sons, or can result in a reason-able adjustment where their relationship continues in a positive way.

A prototypical case that I found in my research reveals the process. A father whose son was five when the parents divorced attempted to maintain his relationship with his son. He stated, "I would see my son once a week in a kind of Christmas situation, where I overloaded him with gifts and his favorite foods, and took him places he wanted to go. My wife, out of the hostility which caused the divorce in the first place, began to undercut me with my son.

"I tried to keep up with his schoolwork—how he was doing and all that—but my ex-wife gave me very little information.

"Then she remarried and I was almost totally blocked out by the new father. I remember calling once when my son was ten. Her new husband yelled out loudly, 'Your ex is on.' Those two bastards began working on my kid. He became very cool and distant. I haven't given up on my relationship to my son, but it is very difficult to keep it going under these circumstances."

In most cases, the role of the mother is greatly enlarged by the divorce and subsequent distancing of the father. In a study by E. Mavis Hetherington, Martha Cox and Roger Cox, forty-eight divorced couples were compared to forty-eight intact couples. They found that in divorces in which children were involved, the mother was awarded custody, except under unusual circumstances. Although the proportion of children living with their divorced father is increasing, in the 1980 population survey by the Census Bureau only 8.4 percent of children of divorced parents were reported to reside with their father. Thus, the most frequently found family condition in the immediate post-divorce situation is one in which a child is living in a home with a single mother and is having intermittent contact with the father.

The study found that in the two months following divorce, divorced fathers, in contrast to fathers in intact homes, spend more time at work, in solitary activities and with friends. They spend less time in recreational activities and in their own homes. The pattern of more working and less time at home is also present at one year and two years after divorce. For many fathers this seems to involve an active effort to avoid solitude and loneliness. Many fathers will do anything to avoid returning to an empty home.

A most important finding of the study was that contact with the divorced father and his son decreased steadily over time. According to the study, the father's contact was motivated by a variety of factors. Sometimes it was based on a deep attachment to a son or continuing attachment to the wife. Often it was based on feelings of duty or attempts to assuage guilt or to maintain a sense of continuity in their lives. Negative reasons for visitations reported by the fathers included the desire to annoy, compete with or retaliate against the spouse.[8]

The divorced mother, who is often cast in the role of both mother and father to compensate for the father's distance, is usually experiencing personal difficulties of her own. Divorced mothers usually have significantly less contact with adults other than their ex-husbands. They develop a sense of being locked into a child's world. In the study, divorced mothers described themselves as prisoners to their children. Of course, this was less true of working mothers than nonworking mothers. Many non-working mothers complained that most of their prior social contacts had been made through professional associates of their husband, and that with divorce these associations terminated.

This "trapped" condition tends to frustrate the divorced mother, and often produces emotional problems. There is evidence that on some unconscious level the mother may act out her problems on the physical representation of her husband in her life—her son. In a psychodrama I ran with a woman who had been divorced about a year, at a critical point in the session she openly admitted that her hostility toward her husband was often displaced onto her son. She said, "They are look-alikes from their faces to their feet. And I can see from this session that the terrible hostility I have toward Jim is something I may take out on Mark, who to me is really Jim, Jr. Look, he comes back from his visits with that bastard and the kid almost sounds like him. The brat begins to criticize me just like Jim used to when we were married!" This woman was aware of the displacement of her aggression toward her husband onto her son. Most women are not. And no doubt their hostility toward their ex-husbands is sometimes unfairly visited on their sons.

One of the most marked changes in divorced fathers in the

first year following divorce is a decline in feelings of competence as a parent. Many men feel they have failed as fathers and husbands and express doubts about future marriage. In addition to these feelings related specifically to marriage, divorced fathers may feel they are coping less well at work, not functioning as well in social situations and are less competent in heterosexual relations. These factors no doubt negatively influence their competence as fathers.

The large body of research on divorced men further reveals that there is a surge of social activity and self-improvement which usually occurs about a year after divorce. This seems to be an attempt to resolve some of the problems related to identity and loss of self-esteem experienced by a divorced father. The most important factor in changes in self-concept two years after divorce is the establishment of a satisfying intimate heterosexual relationship by the father. Fathers who remain divorced tend to have some deficiency in their effectiveness as fathers.

More than 75 percent of divorced people remarry. Since most mothers receive custody of their children, it is logical to assume that over half the families reconstituted after divorce will include a stepfather.

The mores reflect a curious kind of ambivalence rooted in a bias in favor of natural parents rearing their children in an intact home. There is often a negative stereotype surrounding stepparenthood, especially around the stepfather. The stepfather has been pictured, at best, as assuming parental responsibilities out of love for his new wife, with perhaps a gradual warming to the child who was a part of the "package." At worst, he has been depicted as indifferent and callous, or as an exploiter of his wife's children.

Contrary to these stereotypes, many men enact their stepfather role lovingly, in a positive and effective way. The following report by one man reflects the way a stepfather can become the "real" father.

"When I married my wife her children were six and seven. In our family we referred to their biological father as Ralph, his name, and I referred to myself as 'the father' or 'the real father.' Ralph lived in another city and did not visit very often. He had children by both a previous marriage and a subsequent one.

When the kids were in their late teens they each went once to see him, and have had only casual contacts with him since. I became their real father in every way. My son is now in his twenties and we have a wonderful friendship. I love him very much, and the terrible battles we had when he was a teenager pale into insignificance in comparison with the joy and proud feelings I now have about my son. I'm glad I became his *real* father, and not his so-called stepfather."

This stepfather performed his role as the real father in a most positive way. He could do this partly because the biological father stepped out of the picture, and because he had a real love for his adopted children. In many cases, however, the behavior expected of a father is crystal clear when compared with that of the stepfather. The role of stepfather is as yet not clearly defined, and the stepfather has no place to turn for explicit information and guidance about stepfathering.

The sociometry or relationship system of the stepfather's new family situation is usually fraught with problems. His new son may be very protective about his mother, extol the virtues of his own father and have a natural antipathy toward his stepfather. The problems inherent in the stepfather role may be resolved with effective overtime fathering; however, it is usually a difficult role for a person to assume.

Another factor in the relationship between the divorced father and his son is the appearance on the scene of a woman who may become the son's stepmother. She may want only the man, and may perceive his son as a problem she had not bargained for. Perhaps she simply may not want to become a mother. Of course, there is an enormous difference in the situation when the son is living with his father, in contrast with his being alone.

In *The Single Father's Handbook*, Drs. Richard H. Gatley and David Koulack describe some of the problems which may arise when the father introduces a "new companion" into the father-son complex: "Separated fathers experience a lot of complications and difficulties when they begin to establish a close relationship with 'another woman'—some of them imaginary and some very real. Some problems arise for your new relationship because of the various emotional reactions you're likely to go through as a result of separation. Other difficulties more specifically relate to your new companion's reactions to your kids (and to you as a 'father'), as well as your children's responses to her. And finally, as a consequence, there are the complications and problems associated with being caught in the middle between your children and your new companion."[9]

Of course, there is an enormous difference in the situation when the son is living with his father, in contrast to his being alone. One divorced man I interviewed, who lived with his son, described his experience as follows: "My son was sixteen when my wife and I separated. When I began to see other women, I felt a constraint introducing him to someone who was special to me. The women in my life whom I considered unattractive and unintelligent I saw without him. I went to their homes rather than bringing them to our home. Our house was a buddy situation, involving two single 'men' who occasionally entertained women. The situation did provide for a discussion of sexual relationships, and consequently developed into a sexual education situation for both my son and me."

Some sons living with their fathers may be unusual and at an early age have the compassion necessary to be pleased about their fathers' new relationships. Other sons, especially self-centered sons, are jealous of these women and may attempt to the best of their ability to sabotage the relationships.

One divorced man reported to me: "The last five years of my life with my wife were terrible. My son, who was sixteen at the time, saw me sitting around alone a lot while she stepped out. He opted to live with me after the divorce and I was looking forward to a great new time of life.

"At first, when I had some part-time girlfriends, he didn't give me any trouble. In fact when they slept over he would have a sly look on his face as if to say, 'It's great you have someone to sleep with.' However, when I developed a more permanent love affair the trouble began. He seemed jealous of the time I spent with my new love and resented her. He would be cold and distant to her when she was around the house. And sometimes when I came in late he would yell out 'Is she here?' or 'Are you alone?'

"It was difficult to deal with him because you can't punish a kid for his feelings. Basically he would resent anyone who took over the time I would usually spend with him. Needless to say, his response didn't help my relationship with my new girlfriend. To my son's credit, I suspect that on some level he was worried about me and didn't want to see me fall into the terrible marriage trap I had been in with his mother. Mainly, however, his reaction was one of jealousy, as he was very self-centered.

"Fortunately, my girlfriend was a wonderful, understanding woman who understood my son's feelings. Consequently, I didn't find myself in the middle, as might have occurred if she reacted to him differently."

In general, one of the most difficult problems that emerge between a father and son after divorce is the distancing problem that results from the mother's custody of the child. Research reveals that divorced men have special problems; however, they must compensate for their new positions with their sons by spending as much quality time with them as possible. In this regard, my research clearly reveals that most sons love to spend time alone with their fathers and this may occur more frequently after divorce. In some cases this time alone was not available when the father was at home, so the divorce can be a blessing in disguise. A father's special attention to his son's needs, and seeing him alone as often as possible, can often reduce the difficulties of the divorce. In fact, some divorced fathers become more concerned about their sons and develop better relationships with them after divorce than during the days of conflict that existed in their unhappy marriages. The father, on balance, may be in a better emotional state after he accustoms himself to the separation, and he can sometimes relate better to his son from his new life situation.

TEACHERS AND COACHES

In earlier times parents were closely involved in almost all aspects of the socialization of their children. In recent years school and sports have become increasingly significant activities for children, and many former parental responsibilities have been placed in the hands of teachers and coaches. These individuals become significant figures who can comprise intervening variables between father and son. Teachers in particular can become role models for children. As such their value may be positively reinforced or condemned by fathers.

In my son's earlier years I would use his teachers as a reference point for discussing his schoolwork. We often played a role-playing game where I had him reverse roles with his elementary school teacher. This was done because my son, like many children of his age, did not answer *direct* questions. The role-playing can often provide useful information to a father about his son's school situation that can later be of benefit to his child. I would have him play the role of one teacher (who happened to be a man) and then ask: "Mr. Smith, how's Mitch doing in class?"

The essence of Mitch's feelings about his teacher was revealed by the answer: "He's a great reader. He's not too good in math, and sometimes he fools around too much, but he's a fine boy and I like him."

This particular elementary school teacher truly liked Mitch and was an ego booster. When the four of us (his mother was the fourth) were together, Mitch was bathed in a positive glow of three adults who reinforced his positive qualities. He knew of his parents' love for him, but Mr. Smith was a significant other who validated him. In effect, he temporarily became a father surrogate to my son, and I perceived him in that context.

Some of my son's other teachers were not such positive validators of his developing ego, and were, in my opinion, negative surrogate parents. There were a number of cases where my son's teachers were less than logical people whose assessment of him required my intervention in order to change the situation and bolster his ego-development. One case in point was an alcoholic male high school teacher who picked on all his students unmercifully and unfairly. At first I tended to discount my son's presentation of the man because Mitch's description of his behavior was so outrageous. However, after checking it out with other students and meeting the man for a "counseling session" with my son and his adviser, I concluded that my son's perception of the man was valid. When I met the teacher I had an open mind to his possibly constructive criticism about my son's "poor work" in his class. He opened the meeting by saying, "You're not going to be belligerent, are you?" From that point on I treated the emotionally disturbed and somewhat paranoid man with the care required for the deranged. Furthermore, over the balance of the semester, I advised my son on how to deal with people of his type, giving him an object educational experience on how people with emotional problems can get and stay in jobs they shouldn't be in. (The school was aware of the man's problem, but he had tenure and it was felt that there were insufficient grounds for his dismissal.)

My son passed the course and the teacher became an object lesson for considerable positive discussion between my son and me about difficult people. The point is that some fathers automatically but incorrectly take the side of the teachers, thus confusing their sons on how other adults really are. My own parents tended to take that approach with authority figures, supporting negative adults who should not have been teachers in the first place.

The parental roles of training and discipline in contemporary society are often entirely relegated by parents to their children's teachers. Fathers should be aware of the degree to which teachers can have a positive or negative impact on their sons' socialization, and they should perceive their sons' teachers as either negative or positive surrogate parents.

Sometimes an outstanding teacher can help to compensate in the classroom for the negative and destructive behavior of a child's parents at home. In this regard, a well-trained, sensitive elementary school teacher who taught in an urban ghetto school described how children who were having problems at home brought their difficulties into the classroom situation.

"My experiences have been varied, but the number-one problem I confront is discipline when dealing with problem students in violent situations in my classroom. During my first year of teaching, I went through a period of shock. My students were disrespectful and did not want to learn. At least 70 percent of my time was devoted to disciplining them, no doubt to make up for the extremes of discipline that I found existed in their homes. Basically I was dealing with problems in the classroom that emanated from the children's parents. Most of these kids had a mother but no father to discipline them. I had to fill in and discipline for these absentee fathers. Sometimes, when I would try to get a violent child's parent to correct the child's behavior, it would backfire and lead to a more severe problem. One father I called about his son's bad behavior beat him with an extension cord. When I found out about it, I stopped calling that parent. Another time, after calling home about a student's bad behavior, I found out that the boy had been burned with a hot iron by his father. He appeared with welts all over his arms the next day in class."

The classroom situation is besieged by the problems that exist in the children's homes and communities. Because of these problems, the maintenance of discipline becomes a teacher's major objective, and the teacher's primary task of conveying knowledge is subverted. The teacher often finds himself cast as a surrogate parent in a difficult situation.

The coach can be another significant parent surrogate. It is well documented by many dramatic cases that athletic coaches often become significant surrogate fathers to their athletes. There are many testimonials given to such well-known coaches as Knute Rockne, Vince Lombardi and others, who became macho but positive second fathers to their charges. In fact, most coaches are selected for the job because they have fatherly characteristics.

Most coaches are reasonable men who are valuable as father surrogates. However, too many of them are super-macho types who demand superman behavior from their young charges. Their style can often conflict with a boy's father's approach. The conflict between a humanistic father and a macho coach was revealed to me in an incident I observed during a batting session. An eleven-year-old, no doubt both out of fear and lack of skill, kept stepping away from the ball when he swung, and of course he hit air. The whole world was watching. When he came out of the batter's box he was obviously stifling his tears of failure. Finally he couldn't control himself any longer and broke into loud sobs. A nearby coach admonished him, "Come on, kid. For Christ's sake, be a man. Stop crying like a baby."

The child's loving father pushed the coach aside, led the boy to privacy in back of the dugout, hugged him and said, "Okay, pal, go ahead and cry. Screw the coach. If you feel something, express it. There's nothing wrong with a man crying."

Fathers who are also their sons' coaches confront some special situations. The double role as coach and father often causes them to overreact to their sons in a game situation. One devastating case that came to my attention involved a youngster who was picked off at third during a tight game because he took too long to lead off the base. The boy, who incidentally wore a hearing aid, walked dejectedly back to the dugout. He was greeted there by his irate macho coach-father who slapped him twice with his open hand on the head. Fortunately the poor victim was still wearing his batter's helmet, which partially shielded him from this revolting and totally unnecessary attack by his father. This macho father was so concerned with the fact that his ego extension did not perform properly that he humiliated his son and himself in public.

Many macho fathers feel that competitive sports can produce certain results that they feel are of value. One such macho father remarked to me: "What do I hope my son gets out of sports? A sense of competition, a sense of fulfillment and learning skills. I'd like him to learn how to compete. I'm a businessman and I see the world as competitive. A certain amount of competitive spirit is required in life.

"I know that some people say that little league's too competitive and that it puts too much pressure on the kid. But I don't agree. School is competitive. Even in the open-structured too-liberal school that my kids go to, there's still competition. It's natural for a kid to say, 'I'm better than you.' Life is full of competition and the faster a kid learns that, the better off he is, whether it's in little league or life."

The range of emotional impacts on the father-son relationship through athletics was presented to me in an insightful interview I had with a man who effectively enacted the roles of father, coach and umpire. He had a broader perception of the value of sports to a child than macho, competitive, battering fathers.

"Many kids' problems on the field are manifestations of problems at home in their families. On the field many a child is responding to the discipline of a game, when discipline is absent in his home life, especially from his father. He finds on the field a positive structure that's missing in his day-to-day life at home.

"I have seen kids respond effectively to this discipline. There are kids who have deliberately provoked me to kick them out of a ball game I was umpiring. I can think of a very specific case of two youngsters, products of a broken home, living in a completely disorganized manner. The marriage was gone. Both parents apparently had abandoned the children, who were living with their grandparents. I don't have to tell you how generous grandparents can be. They tend to spoil children. And that's exactly what I saw there. One youngster was constantly cutting up. He was doing everything—throwing the ball away, throwing his helmet in the air, letting loose with displays of temper which I guess he was permitted to get away with at home. One day I threw him out of the game. He threw his helmet away and I told him to get out of the ball game. It was as if a safe had fallen on him. It was the first time in years that somebody had said, 'This is as far as you're going to go—no further.' The next week, not only did he play without an incident but he came over after his game and offered to keep score. So that week and in subsequent weeks I was looking at a different boy. He was challenging me, he was testing me, and I responded. A lot of parents, both mothers and fathers, bring their kids here to get another adult to do a job with their kids. We become surrogate fathers to these boys.

"My own son was born with clubfeet and I coached because I thought baseball might help him. His toes were formed but the feet faced each other and there was only so much that could be done medically. He was somewhat handicapped—not as severely as many kids, but he spent many years in one hospital after another. At first, when my wife and I saw him hit a ball and run the bases, it was an enormous feeling. Finally we took it for granted. He was determined that this was going to work, and slowly, slowly, those feet straightened out as he ran the base-paths."

I was a little league parent for five years, and then I coached a team. During that period I had one major focus of concern, my son's emotional and physical well-being in little league. At times I worried about him sliding or being hit by a ball. And I worried constantly about the emotional impact on my son of being benched, devalued or overly berated by a coach.

In my own role as coach, I was surprised to discover that many of the kids related to me as they probably did to their own fathers. Some kids cowered before me for no reason other than that they transferred onto me their past conditioning with their own macho fathers. The boys who related closely and lovingly to their own fathers almost immediately related to me openly, with humor, and with a certain amount of warmth which was touching. These were youngsters who I later confirmed had loving-doubling fathers. The league I coached in was in an affluent section of Los Angeles. The children of ego-centered parents were kids who were very demanding. They would tell me what position they should play, and about my errors in judgment. When they did show up at a game, which was rare, the fathers would be overdressed for the occasion—and they too would, without any solicitation on my part, brashly evaluate my performance as a coach, and give me orders. It became apparent to me during the year I coached how closely sons resemble their fathers emotionally.

Interaction between fathers and sons is clearly modified for good or bad by the relevant others in their social configuration. The most notable intervening variable and filtering person is the wife-mother. If she is a positive nurturing person, her son will develop a positive image of women. An effective mother can have a significant impact on a son's image of his father.

All families, especially in our complex society, have other intervening community people who can become a useful part of the relationship between father and son. Stepparents, teachers and coaches can be positively woven into the tapestry of the family configuration—when proper communication exists, and there is compassion and goodwill.

Fathers and sons should be conscious of the impact of past generations of men in a family's lineage. A grandfather can be viewed as a person with wisdom who is a viable link to the family's roots. He is not only one of the family's most significant historians, he can also contribute as a conflict-free extra parent to his grandson. A man can see through his grandfather where

CHAPTER FIVE

Special Problems: Normal and Pathological

HERE ARE NORMAL transitory problems that exist for fathers and
ns, long-term serious problems and special unanticipated
oblems. Normal transitory problems emerge especially in the
n's teenage years. This type of problem basically stems from a
n's needs to separate his self from his father's self, and to
dividuate. It is also normal for fathers and sons to see certain
ues entirely differently because they perceive life from two
fferent cultural viewpoints, that of an older man and that of a
enager.

When such normal transitory problems are not handled logi-
lly and effectively, conflict between a father and son can be
acerbated into a lifelong serious struggle that can enervate and
bilitate both parties. For example, if during the teenage years
hers and sons improperly handle what is most often simple
perimentation with drugs, alcohol or a minor act of delin-
ency, a normal transitory problem can be escalated into a
ajor lifelong problem.

In my experience working with drug addicts and criminals, I
ve traced back parental overreaction or overkill punishment
a factor in contributing to later more serious crimes. In brief,
e action and reaction of father and son can minimize a prob-
n and make it transitory, or can have the effect of pouring fuel
a small fire and escalating into a major conflagration. The
ulting struggle often results in emotional disorders, drug
use, juvenile delinquency or criminality.

he's been and what he may become in his later y
father can also serve as a vital arbiter of family iss
philosophical force in the boy's life and serve a:
both to him and his father.

Unquestionably the entire cast of others in a fat
life drama affects their relationship. However, th
ther can and should orchestrate the way in whic
interact with him and his son in their real-life psy

DEVIANCE AND EMOTIONAL DISORDERS

There are several father-son configurations which can produce delinquency in a son. The simplest situation is illustrated by the old saying, "Like father, like son," where the son is "a chip off the old block." Criminal fathers are likely to produce criminal sons.

There are criminogenic families which are almost certain to produce delinquent children. This negative inheritance factor is not restricted to poor families living in depressed ghettos. White-collar criminals who live in upper socioeconomic neighborhoods also produce deviant sons with emotional problems.

There are many factors that produce delinquent youths. However, a considerable amount of research into delinquency reveals the fact that the disciplinary process, as it relates to the father-son relationship, is a significant pivotal factor.

One study that confirms this fact is the delinquency research of Elinore and Sheldon Glueck. Their research compared 500 delinquent boys to a control group of 500 nondelinquents. Their major finding was that delinquents were treated significantly differently from nondelinquents in terms of discipline.

They defined the categories of discipline practices as follows: (1) sound, consistent and firm control of the boy by the father, but not so strict as to arouse fear and antagonism; (2) fair control which is indefinite—sometimes strict, sometimes lax; (3) unsound, extremely lax or extremely rigid control by the father, which on the one hand gives the boy unrestrained freedom of action and on the other restricts him to the point of rebellion.

The Gluecks found with regard to the disciplinary process in their delinquent cases that 2.5 percent were considered sound, 27.4 percent fair and 70.1 percent unsound. Discipline by the father was therefore found to be a crucial interaction pattern in the development of a son's delinquent behavior patterns.[1]

A father needs to be consistent in his disciplinary approach if controls are to be adequately internalized into his son's personality. Situations and appropriate methods of dealing with them must recur regularly enough to let a boy develop proper concepts of conduct and be able to distinguish suitable and unsuitable responses. If the process is handled correctly by the father, the son will internalize proper values.

There is a considerable amount of research that reveals that fathers can have more of a deleterious impact than mothers and therefore may be more responsible for producing juvenile delinquency. One study concluded that sons who feel their fathers love them are less likely to become delinquent than sons who do not feel love from their fathers. An important aspect of the socialization process and an apparent insulator against delinquency is a high emotional *quality* of love demonstrated by a father toward his son.

Robert G. Andry carried out an in-depth study of delinquency and the parental factor of father love. His research explored the quality of parental affection and love as it related to youths who became delinquent or remained nondelinquent. Delinquents and nondelinquents were radically differentiated in their feelings as to the adequacy of the affective roles of the parents. Delinquents tended to feel that their fathers didn't love them and did not care about them, whereas nondelinquents tended to feel loved by both parents. Moreover, Andry's research indicated that delinquent boys felt that their fathers would be embarrassed if they were to show open affection for their sons. Most nondelinquents in the sample felt that their fathers cared and openly showed love. Therefore, the prime differentiating feature between delinquents and nondelinquents with regard to their parents was the delinquents' negative perceptions of their fathers and their feeling that their fathers gave them little in the way of love and caring.[2]

Cold, inconsistent and inappropriate behavior by a father toward his son usually emanates from the fact that the father is besieged by his own problems. The pattern in many cases operates psychodynamically as follows: the father, inundated by his own difficulties, has a tendency to put off and ignore his son's needs for normal discipline and control. The son gets out of hand, partly because he has no clear direction and partly in the acting out of normal rebellious behavior. The father decides he has to enact his father role, partly because of his own ego needs and not because of the requirements of his son's behavior. Out of his own frustration and problems, and in an effort to make up for his past laxness, he assumes his controlling-father role with venom. He resorts to extreme disciplinary action that is inappropriate to his son's immediate misbehavior. The process often involves behavior that crosses the fine line between severe discipline and hysterical and pathological child-battering.

The type of father who is most apt to produce a delinquent or neurotic son is one who does not "make the punishment fit the crime." The father's response to his son's misdeeds is erratic, and may range from zero to overkill. The father's own disturbed personality needs become more of a force in determining his discipline than the nature of the son's deviance.

Whatever their basic father style, fathers who discipline in this fashion are inconsistent, irrational and ineffectual. The son is not in interaction with a loving human being who is trying to show him the correct way to live. He is quite apt to respond with fear and rebellion to this type of effort at socializing him. The son becomes rebellious, estranged and alienated from his father and consequently from society.

Many studies of the causes of various patterns of violent behavior reveal a correlation between brutal fathers and violent sons. The use of harsh discipline by a father to socialize his son is often a significant factor in producing a violent society.

Data on child-battering reveal that over 700 American children are killed, over 100,000 are severely battered and 50,000 to 75,000 are sexually abused every year, mainly by their fathers. The tragic results of these appalling statistics are graphically illustrated in daily newspaper headlines that report on criminals such as the "Hillside Stranglers," the "Freeway Murderers" and others among the increasingly commonplace killers and muggers of our time. Most individuals of this type were victims of child-battering fathers, who replicate the sins of their fathers.

Disciplinary child-battering by psychopathic macho fathers takes many diverse forms; however, the extreme case often brings the dynamics of the interaction between a father and a son into sharper focus. The following case illustrates this extreme. Ralph, at eighteen, was in custody for attempting to kill his father. At the time I met Ralph, he was in a mental hospital and was diagnosed as schizophrenic. The verbal interactions he had with various therapists in the hospital about his past behavior (which we learned through psychodrama was constantly on his mind) had admittedly been of limited help in reaching him. His personal therapist had participated in several psychodrama sessions and requested that I direct a session with Ralph to help him explore some of Ralph's psychodynamics in action. Ralph's therapist was present at all of the sessions and very productively followed the leads we produced in our psychodramas in his private therapeutic sessions with Ralph.

In addition to Ralph's potential for acting out his murderous feelings, another symptom that he manifested was a body tic. When it was active his body would writhe in an epileptic fashion. The tic usually seemed to appear whenever he felt anger or was under pressure. According to a medical report by a doctor who had examined Ralph, there appeared to be no physiological basis for the tic. In the first psychodrama session I ran with Ralph as the protagonist, I noted that the tic appeared and became quite pronounced whenever there was any reference to his father— even when the word "father" was spoken by a member of the group.

In the session Ralph led us back to the basic and traumatic scenes in his life with his father. Most of them revolved around severe discipline by his father. He acted out a horrendous situation that occurred when he was eight. His father had punished him by tying him by his hands to a ceiling beam in their cellar, like meat on a hook, and then beating him with a heavy board.

Ralph related his father's erratic pattern of discipline: "Most of the time my father was okay with me. In fact, he seldom bothered me. Then it was like he would go nuts and start hitting me for no reason. Sometimes I would screw up at school and he'd get a note, look at it and throw it away. Other times the slightest thing would have him screaming at me and hitting me really hard with his fists."

We determined from several sessions with Ralph, and my consultations with his therapist, that traumatic experiences had produced Ralph's tic, which had always appeared after a particularly horrendous beating. It seemed to be a way he controlled the desire to strike back at his father. Ralph had two extreme postures that emerged from his father's erratic and overkill behavior; one was the tic, which in effect was a turning inward of his anger which enabled him to restrain himself from hitting back; and the other was uncontrolled violence. Other sessions with Ralph revealed that his hostility toward his father was displaced onto others, especially other children at school, where he was often in fights.

In relating Ralph's plight, it is apparent that the abuse he was subjected to by his father and his symptomatic responses were severe ones. It is important to bear in mind that the battered child syndrome is both physical and emotional and is *a matter of degree*. Although very few children are exposed to the extreme physical punishment that Ralph was, many have experienced some type of negative socialization and have developed symptoms of rage, negative personality postures and self-destructive tendencies in direct response to the negative causal factors in their lives. In my work in psychodrama, I have seen many levels of intensity and patterns similar to Ralph's parental syndrome in people who, for the most part, are normal functioning members of society.

The father who had Ralph hospitalized was obviously the arch object of Ralph's hatred. Ralph could seldom talk to his father in life. He would either manifest the incapacitating tic, run away or, as he finally did, attempt to kill him.

In the final scene of one psychodrama, we had progressed to a point where he accepted a male nurse as an auxiliary ego in the role of his father. In the scene, Ralph alternately produced the tic or attempted to attack his "father," as played by the nurse. There was hardly any verbalization of Ralph's rage—he required actions to express his emotions.

After Ralph had physically acted out much of his rage, I finally improvised a vehicle that facilitated a conversation between Ralph and the man who played his father. I put a table between him and his psychodramatic father. At the same time he talked to his "father," I gave him the option and the freedom to punch a pillow that he accepted symbolically as his father. This combination of psychodrama devices enabled Ralph to structure in thought and put into words the deep venom which had resulted from his father's treatment of him. He blurted out much of his long-repressed hatred in a lengthy diatribe. Finally, we removed the props, and after his rage was spent by hitting his "father" with a battoca, he fell into his "father's" arms and began to sob. "Why did you have to beat me like that, Dad? Don't you know how much I love you and need you?"

Although he went through several phases of his hostility in several sessions, he could not go all the way and forgive his father, a symbolic act that I had determined from many sessions would help to relieve him of the core of hostility that had produced his violent acting-out behavior.

In later sessions we had Ralph play the role of his father, and surprisingly he knew that the same violent syndrome had been experienced by his father with *his* father. For the first time Ralph began to empathize with the early experiences in his father's life that had brutalized him. Ralph's grandfather, who had also beaten his son, was a link in a chain of generations of fatherly violence toward sons. Ralph was indirectly receiving the fallout of his father's anger toward his own father, or Ralph's grandfather. When Ralph reversed roles and returned to being himself, his hostility toward his father was diminished, and, psychodramatically at least, he forgave him that day.

All of the material acted out in the psychodrama sessions was more closely examined in his private sessions with his therapist. In addition, I had a number of productive discussions with both Ralph and his therapist on an individual basis. This combination of therapeutic activities seemed to be most effective in helping Ralph solve his emotional problems. In my follow-up of Ralph's case, I learned that he had made a reasonable adjustment after leaving the hospital, due to a combination of our therapeutic work and his understanding of the source of his violent emotions. He stayed clear of his father because he still couldn't handle that relationship. The positive results were that he went to work, married at twenty and, according to the reports I received, for the most part established a reasonable life situation.

Most male delinquents have either absent, distant fathers or fathers who do not have a resonant relationship with their sons. The lack of compatibility between the delinquent father and son can usually be found in the dynamics of their unsound, ineffectual disciplinary relationship. The consistency, intensity and quality of the disciplinary process between a delinquent father and son is usually unsound.

Hypocrisy is another element through which a father can foster deviance in his son. Fathers often reinforce their sons' deviant behavior by telling their sons to "do as I say, not as I do." In this context I once observed a fifteen-year-old delinquent boy in Juvenile Hall talking to his father on visiting day. After chastising his son for being in jail, the father gave his son a report on himself and how his life was going. The conversation was dominated by the father relating to his son his latest physical altercations. He told his son how he had assaulted a neighbor when the latter had requested that he move his car because it was partially blocking the driveway. The boy's eyes glowed as his father related his macho adventures in great detail. The boy was in Juvenile Hall for gang activity, specifically an assault he had committed on a boy who was then in critical condition in the hospital. The father hypocritically admonished his son for his acts of violence in the gang. In the double message from the father, the father's own violent exploits were heard louder and clearer than his admonitions against gang violence.

Many creative individuals commit deviant acts in their early years, and go on to adulthood to become creative, productive people. Regrettably, overrestrictive fathers, whose definitions for correct behavior are too stringent, can propel their children into deviant behavior by labeling them delinquent, and thus bring the forces of the administration to bear on them. This process can foster and then confirm a self-concept of delinquency in a son.

In my work in juvenile detention, I have seen grossly disparate responses by fathers to the same behavior. I have seen fathers petition for their sons to be locked up for what amounted to simple arrogance. I have seen fathers who defended their sons' atrocious assaults. The definition of the same act by different fathers can be enormously varied. In this context I strongly recommend that a father determine the true seriousness of an act before responding too extremely to his child's behavior. The father may be out of touch with community values. In such cases the child feels wronged by his father.

The labeling of a child as a delinquent or suffering from an emotional disorder is too often the result of a judge's bias or the socioeconomic position of the father. Lower-class children who misbehave are more apt to be classified as delinquents, almost regardless of their emotional condition. Children from a more affluent position in the system are more likely to have fathers who intervene in the judicial process, have their sons defined as suffering from emotional problems and acquire the services of a therapist. Because of these factors, especially the intervention of the father, the same deviant behavior by different boys is handled differently by the system.

Drug use and abuse reflects a special aspect of this issue. Children of the affluent who use drugs in their "golden ghettos" are less likely to be arrested than poor children in their ghettos. The power of an affluent father is likely to have great influence on the consequences of his son's drug-use behavior.

ALCOHOL AND DRUG ABUSE

Many sons grasp an escape from the problems they are having with their fathers by indulging in alcohol and drug abuse. Their problems are, at least temporarily, solved by drugs. Drugs are an available escape hatch that cuts across all socioeconomic barriers.

In general, one of the most significant influences of a father on the amount of a son's drug use and abuse is the drug-use habit of the father himself. A father's abstinence creates a healthy role model and a powerful weapon of control over his son. In contrast, a father's drug use is almost a mandate to his son to use drugs. The father who uses drugs and commands his son to abstain is a hypocrite. The father with a drink in his hand and a cigarette in his mouth (his drugs) lecturing his son on the evils of alcohol, pot and pills (the son's substances), is in too weak a position to control his son's drug use.

Some fathers who are addicts tend to use their sons as scapegoats to rationalize their behavior. I vividly recall a complex case I worked on in psychodrama where a father's alcoholism and the family dynamics produced a severe pathology in the son. Herbie, age eleven, came to Dr. J. L. Moreno's Beacon Sanitorium after spending a brief period at a state hospital where he was diagnosed as psychotic.

I worked with Dr. Moreno as an auxiliary ego in several sessions he directed with this frail, supersensitive youngster. Herbie was in an almost constant catatonic state of withdrawal throughout his first session, during which I played the role of his father. Finally, Herbie began to open up and express his enormous hostility toward me as his father. The most productive information was revealed in several devastating cameo statements he made when he reversed roles with me and assumed the role of his drunken father. The manner in which Herbie was typecast in the "sick" role by his father is indicated by his father's harangues to him. Summarizing many sessions, these essentially were his father's and mother's messages to Herbie:

HERBIE AS HIS FATHER: You little bastard, I never wanted you in the first place. If you weren't such a goddamn problem, I would quit drinking. *You made me an alcoholic!* Because of *you* I can't even hold a job. You've ruined our family.

Herbie's mother was also a significant negative force in driving him out of his world of painful reality into a withdrawn dreamworld where he was cast as a psychotic.

HERBIE AS MOTHER: I love you, my sweet boy. I feel awful about what's happening to you. But really, if it weren't for you I'd still have my husband. After you were born everything went wrong. It's not your fault but you were a mistake. Your dad wasn't ready to be a father. He drinks because of you and the problems you give him.

In this triad (there were no other children), the parents unfairly projected their problems, especially the father's alcoholism, onto Herbie in an effort to rationalize their own deficiencies. Because of their need to hold on to their rationalizations the parents unconsciously had a vested interest in keeping Herbie in the "sick" role despite their overt protestations to the contrary. If Herbie was "sick," they could rationalize their own behavior by blaming *him* for their problems. Herbie's reaction to this unbearable pressure was to retreat from the painful world of his family's reality into a cocoon of fantasy, his psychotic state.

In a variety of psychodrama sessions with his parents which included discussions of Herbie's feelings about them, Herbie's problems were somewhat relieved. When the family pressure was taken off Herbie by means of placement in a reasonable foster-family setting, he made considerable progress in the resolution of his problems. Without Herbie to blame, the parents had to seek help for their problems. And without his mother and father, other more constructive role possibilities opened up for Herbie. *It is vital to understand the social atom of an individual, the roles he is cast in and the sociometry of the family to understand any member's emotional illness.* In this case, the alcoholism of the father was an issue affecting in a circuitous way his son's mental health.

A father's overreaction to his son's drug use can often produce unnecessary conflict and exacerbate the problem. As a case in point, one young man described how his moderate drug use caused severe conflict with his father.

"When I was in junior high school I began to fool around with grass like all the other kids I knew. I also dropped acid a few times. One day I came home and my father was in a frenzy. He had found some grass in my room. He blew up and began screaming at me like a real nut, calling me a drug addict. I felt he was ridiculous and tried to explain that all the kids did it and it was no big thing. Also I was really pissed that he went into my room without asking me. We were just yelling and my mother was trying to keep him cool, but he got madder and madder. Finally he hit me. I started out the door and told him to go fuck himself. That did it. He really started to hit me like a crazy man.

"I went over to a friend and I was so upset I smoked a joint to calm myself down. From then on until I was eighteen and had moved out, my life at home with my father was one big battle.

"Even when we talked calmly, which happened a few times with a therapist, we never saw eye to eye. He saw grass as the devil's weed and I saw it as a mild drug that I really liked. Actually, I hardly smoke anymore. I'm busy at college and with my life. I use it less and less. But my old man and I to this day hassle about it."

It is apparent here that the father's extreme viewpoint on a contemporary commonplace drug-use activity produced an unnecessary conflict between this father and son. I am not implying that fathers should condone or accept their sons' drug usage if it does not conform to their own values. However, an overkill attitude as indicated in the foregoing case can drive an unnecessary wedge into a father-son relationship, and in some cases this can drive a son from drug *use* into drug *abuse*.

The best procedure for a father to follow is to attempt to understand the intensity of his son's usage, keep their lines of communication open and proselytize one's position to the best of the father's ability—using whatever valid facts about the general problem he can glean from existing research. The worst thing a father can do is destroy the sacred relationship he should have with his son. It can lead to more intensive abuse by the son and many painful years for both father and son.

The case of a young man who became a heroin addict reveals how a father and son can engage in a nonproductive struggle for many years because of the father's disciplinary overkill. I first met the son, Al, when he was in his early thirties, at a drug rehabilitation center where I directed weekly therapy sessions. He was there to deal with a heroin addiction problem that had not been resolved, as he put it, "by the best psychiatric minds in the Western world." Al's father was a wealthy dentist, and he grew up in a relatively affluent home in New York. Al was a college graduate and for various periods in his life a "speed freak" and a heroin addict.

Al was a highly intelligent man with a flair for the absurd. He once told me a story about the last days of his "speed" (amphetamine) habit: "When the police came to take me away to jail I simply couldn't understand why they wouldn't wait until I cleaned the last few half-dollar-sized tiles in my bathroom. After all, I had cleaned and polished all the others with my toothbrush."

Al went for help for what he and everyone perceived as a heroin problem. Fundamentally, it really was a father-son problem. In a series of group sessions I ran with a small group of residents of the center on the family roots of their drug problems, Al revealed his father problem. Basically his father wanted him to become a dentist like himself, and being a dentist was the last thing in the world Al wanted to do. Al's egocentric father totally intimidated him, and he was full of fear of his father's wrath, which was explosive and physical. His father battered him on many occasions when he was a child. A fear of his father followed him through most of his life and was largely responsible for his becoming a drug addict. Al's father was a perfectionist, and Al always sought, but never got, his father's approval. The only way he might have received his father's approval would have been by becoming a dentist. Al resisted this, because "I never want to become anything like my father."

In one session we allowed Al to express his rage toward his father by psychodramatically killing him with a rolled-up newspaper (used as a knife) in order for him to explore the extent of his hostility. As he plunged the "knife" time and time again into his father, he repeated his basic complaints against him. "Why did you always tell me to be the best? Nothing I did was ever good enough for you. You never approved of anything I did. The drugs help kill the pain of the failure trip you laid on me. I could never live up to your perfectionist standards."

In a final scene of Al's psychodrama with his father, I had him encounter a compassionate "father" who listened to his son. Al finally made the following analytic statement about their relationship. "Dad, I guess you always wanted me to be someone I'm not. And I guess I always wanted you to be someone you're not. And because of that we've never known each other."

Al's father's fixated demands for perfectionist behavior from his son, combined with his dream that his son become a dentist like him, discounted Al as a person with goals and feelings of his own. The son's rebellious drug-addict behavior totally destroyed his father's dreams for his son, and Al used drugs to kill the psychological pain he felt because of the conflict and the constant harangues from his father. In a later discussion on Al's session, one former drug addict in the group said to him, "You can't get milk from a dry tit."

Al replied, "But my father had the only tit I wanted milk from."

It is a sad commentary on many father-son relationships that the two are locked into mortal combat, desiring things from each other that neither can give. The result is often the acting out of deviant behavior that is destructive to both father and son.

HOMOSEXUALITY AND THE FATHER-SON SITUATION

In my work in group psychotherapy, I ran many sessions around the theme of homosexuality. In my earlier (pre-1965) sessions, most homosexuals came into therapy with the basic goal of becoming heterosexual; they perceived their homosexuality with shame as an emotional problem. In the late 1960s, the term "gay" become widespread, more people came out of the closet and homosexuality became viewed as it is now, as more of a sexual preference than a problem. In accordance with this change, the American Psychiatric Association eliminated homosexuality from its list of pathologies.

Fathers are significant determiners of their sons' sexual preferences. In my earlier work I invariably seemed to find that homosexual males had distant fathers and identified with their mothers and other female figures, such as aunts and sisters, in their lives. My simplistic observation was that their unrequited love for their fathers was enacted by identifying with a female attitude toward life, and the men in their lives were substitutes for cold, distant, unloving fathers (psychopathic and egocentric fathers) to whom they could not relate.

An extensive research project in psychoanalysis which compared homosexual and nonhomosexual men concluded that in the majority of cases the behavior of the mothers of homosexuals toward their sons was seductive and overindulgent, while the behavior of their fathers was hostile, ambivalent or indifferent.

The study by Dr. I. Bieber compared eighty-three self-confessed homosexual men with eighty-four married men and concluded that homosexual men, more frequently than heterosexual men, "(1) had unsatisfactory relations with their fathers in childhood; (2) were strongly attached to their mothers in childhood; (3) were overprotected and overindulged by their mothers in childhood; (4) had fathers who were weak and ineffectual as parents; (5) had mothers who were competent as parents; (6) did not want to model themselves after their fathers; (7) wanted to model themselves on their mothers."[3]

The researchers also concluded that

> The disparities between the childhood experiences of homosexuals and heterosexuals are due to their fathers and not to their mothers. The responses indicate that, in the recollections of their sons, more fathers of the homosexuals than those of the married men had weak personalities and were ineffectual as parents, while they do not show that the mothers of the married men had weaker personalities or were less competent than the mothers of the homosexuals. The present results therefore support the contention that homosexual men tend to have weak and ineffectual fathers, but they do not support the belief that their mothers have particularly decisive personalities. . . .
>
> Significantly more homosexual than married men had thought that their fathers had undesirable personality traits and had not wanted to become like their fathers. The married men objected to their fathers' occupations rather than their personalities. The findings are consistent in suggesting that the reason why homosexuals are relatively much more attached to their mothers than to their fathers is not that they have much stronger relationships with their mothers than have heterosexuals, but that they have much poorer relationships with their fathers.[4]

A study by Brian Miller involved in-depth interviews conducted with a sample of forty gay fathers and fourteen of their children. Miller examined the nature and quality of the fathering as experienced by both the fathers and their offspring, and various issues often raised in gay-parent custody cases. His data indicated that notions about gay fathers' compensatory behavior, molestation of children, negative influence on child development and instigation of harassment were largely unfounded. Surprisingly, he also found that the father's "coming out" to his children tended to relieve family tension and strengthen the father-child bond.[5]

A popular viewpoint asserts that homosexual men who have children do so only to hide their true orientation. It is claimed

that these men regard their children merely as smokescreens—
that they have little father affection and that they make poor
parents. Evidence from Miller's study refuted these claims. Gay
fathers do not have children to hide their homosexuality. At the
time they became parents, most of the men did not consider
themselves homosexuals. They had had sexual contacts with
other males, but they did not recognize these experiences as a
salient aspect of their identity or behavior. Instead, they defined
themselves as heterosexuals or tentatively bisexual. Most men
married and became fathers in good faith, reporting genuine
love for their wives and children. Only during the course of their
marriages did the men gradually come to recognize that their
sexual preferences were basically homosexual.

In general, the factors that produce homosexuality in men are
not crystal clear or uniform. I believe that some men turn to
other men because they have controlling, powerful mothers and
distant, weak, poor role models for fathers. Obviously, however,
there are many men who experience this parental configuration
and become heterosexual.

One fact is clear, however: most fathers have a cognitive map
for their sons that includes heterosexuality. This hope is apt to
be expressed by both homosexual and heterosexual fathers, since
being gay involves confronting many prejudices and problems in
our predominantly heterosexual society.

FATHER-SON HEALTH PROBLEMS

Most of the foregoing problems are reflective of emotional
issues that develop between fathers and sons. Often a family is
plagued by a lifelong physical condition that is not the family's
fault in any way, yet can result in emotional problems if not
handled properly. The manner in which severe health problems
are handled can significantly affect the family in general, and
the father and son in particular.

There are reports of extraordinary cases where a father will
literally rescue his son from a second-rate life because of a physical disability and propel him into a life of importance. Theodore
Roosevelt's father cradled his son in his arms for nights on end

when he was a child to support him and give him hope through a severe illness. The man who went on to become a Rough Rider and a great president credits his father in his biography with giving him the courage to succeed by helping him through the dark days of his illness.

Despite the fact that there are many cases of successful recoveries from severe illnesses, there are many other cases where a father and son have to come to terms with a lifelong situation. In such cases the father or son, or both, must make a basic adjustment in his dream map of the other. A major problem arises in the relationship when the exorbitant demands or expectations of the other are not pared down to conform to reality.

In one interview I had with the mother of a brain-damaged child, she told me the following: "My fifteen-year-old son Ron functions at a six-year-old level intellectually and physically. It took me many hours of therapy and emotional upheaval to come to terms with this fact of life. When he was ten I concluded that for the sake of my other son and the resultant drag on our family life, Ron would be better off in an institution. What I really mean is that *all* of us would be better off if he were in an institution. I know this sounds cold, but I felt we had to bite the bullet and do it.

"My husband, I have to say—and remember, this is my opinion—has never faced the problem. He's a businessman and a workaholic. He ignores Ron. He ignores the child's problem, and when I brought up the issue five years ago he didn't want to talk about it. To my knowledge he never tells anyone about Ron's problems. He simply acts as if they don't exist. Our other son, Phil, is two years older than Ron and he's okay physically. My husband has pushed him beyond belief into sports and all kinds of macho activities—camping, hunting. A therapist told me it's clearly a case of his compensating for the son he looks at as defective. . . .

"No, he won't see a therapist about his obvious problem. He has blinders on and absolutely won't look at the reality.

"He doesn't want Ron around but he won't accept my putting him into an institution because that would make a definite statement about our son's retarded condition.

178

"Because of this constant effect on our lives we really have no marriage or sex life. It just goes on day after day with my husband gone most of the time. I take care of Ron as best I can. As soon as my oldest son is eighteen this family will end. I think our marriage died the day we found out about Ron's problem and my husband put on his blinders."

Obviously, the husband, who has not faced the problem, would not grant me an interview. He refuses to accept the reality of a situation which is as much his problem as his son's.

Most fathers with this problem do not respond with such extreme denial. One courageous man who confronted his son's problem, diagnosed as autism, was writer Josh Greenfeld. In his two books, *A Child Called Noah* and *A Place for Noah*, Greenfeld, a perceptive observer and writer, kept a chronicle of his son's behavior and his own reactions. In *A Place for Noah* he describes his son's behavioral problem and his emotional reaction to the situation:

Many people wonder what to name their baby. I still don't know what to call my eleven-year-old son. It is six years since I wrote *A Child Called Noah*. My son was then five years old and had finally seemed to achieve that great pinnacle, toilet training. He was capable of a few words of reward-induced imitative speech, but generally behaved pretty much like a one-year-old with poor sleeping habits and bizarre wakeful activities. His idea of play was flexing and unflexing his hands before his eyes, picking at infinitesimal shreds of lint on the floor, and bouncing up and down on sofas and couches and beds—or endlessly rocking. He seldom interacted with anybody or anything. . . .

I no longer consider—or call—my son Noah autistic. This does not mean his condition has improved markedly. It does mean, however, that my perception of his condition has clarified immeasurably. And I no longer distract myself with the use of a term that implies meaning but defies definition. The word *autism* means self-involved—and who isn't?

My son Noah was—and is—brain-damaged. He suffers from severe developmental disabilities and acute deprivation in his fine motor processes; he is definitely mentally retarded and naturally has a behavior problem. We have yet to discover the exact reasons—which area of the brain and what perceptional faculties are not functioning properly. . . .

Books and articles keep crossing my desk, rhapsodizing over various cures encountered or uncovered. In recent years I have witnessed some changes for the better—and some changes for the worse—in many brain-damaged children, but I have yet to see the evidence of any single dramatic cure with my own eyes. . . .

How is my son Noah now? He is doing better than he has done, but not as well as I would have hoped. If I had once seen his malady as transient, I now know it to be permanent. But I still must deal with it on a transient—or existential—basis. I still both enjoy Noah and endure him. Which is, after all, the way most of us fundamentally treat one another.[6]

Like Mr. Greenfeld, all fathers enjoy and endure their sons, even when they have no special problems. The difference, however, is in the degree of enjoyment and the degree of endurance. Mr. Greenfeld has apparently confronted the reality of the situation and his feelings. No one can say whether the first father's denial of his son's disability is more or less painful than confronting the reality of having a son who doesn't fulfill a father's dream plan.

Another father I interviewed slowly discovered as his son grew up that the adopted boy he had come to love intensely suffered from epilepsy, combined with the possibility of mental retardation.

"We adopted our son Joel when he was eight months old. We noticed something wrong in his early years. He seldom fought for himself, but he was a cheerful, cute, nice kid. He was always a little behind in school and at about nine we had him tested by a doctor who told us that he was educationally handicapped. It was around then that I began to deal with my deeper feelings. My hopes for him to become someone special in the world, someone who was intellectually capable, looked bleak. But I wasn't ready yet to have him fail, or, better said, I wasn't ready to admit that I had failed with him.

"Between the ages of nine and thirteen, he went to a special school. I hated the school because it was a clear symbol and admission that my son had this handicap. My heart sank when he came home one day from school and said, 'Dad, am I really retarded, or some kind of moron?' I began to assure him he was okay and persisted with my myth about him, that he only had a temporary problem.

"In an act of defiance of the reality of his subtle retardation, when he was around thirteen I pulled him out of this special school and put him in a public school. It didn't change the problem.

"A major difficulty I had with him was connected to discipline. I felt sorry for him and hated myself when I yelled at him. But I knew I had to set limits for his own good. Part of the disciplinary problem was that you can yell at a normal kid and call him stupid. But with a kid like mine, if you lose your temper and say that to him, it's devastating.

"At sixteen he had a seizure and we clearly knew he was epileptic. That and symptoms of mental retardation and emotional backwardness are mixed together—and with all the doctors he's been to no one has adequately sorted his problem out to my satisfaction.

"There are, of course, always two problems: his and mine. If I put him in an institution, would it be because it would be better for me or for him? I wouldn't do that because I would feel awful, and if I did, it would clearly mean *I* had failed. It's a dilemma I'm sure all fathers with kids like mine face.

"I think most fathers will do what feels best for them. The fathers I read about like Josh Greenfeld just won't give up on their kids. He, of course, loves him and doesn't want to put him in an institution.

"I always have this poignant flashback of my early childhood. In my neighborhood there was a little man we'd see who was always with his crazy-looking son. They would seldom be seen alone. They were always together, hand in hand. The poor kid had been hit on the head with a baseball bat at the age of eleven and he just stopped growing in every way, physically and emotionally. I remember that father and son—always together walking down the street.

"I now realize in a way I'm that father. And one of my biggest concerns about Joel, who is now twenty-three, is what will happen to him when I'm gone. How will he be taken care of? I still haven't given up hoping that he'll be okay, even though I know he won't. You see, I really love my boy and I'll never give up on my hopes for my son as long as I live."

Fathers, of course, also have physical disabilities that can lead to father-son problems. In one detailed case, psychologist Eric Bermann, in his book, *Scapegoat*, described how an eight-year-old boy's personal problems and subsequent delinquent behavior resulted from an effort to repress the family's general problem produced by his father's terminal illness.

In his work with the family Dr. Bermann learned that the father attempted to conceal the fact that he had a severe heart condition, was in need of open-heart surgery, and was medically considered "close to death" for many years. The family repressed their awareness of the condition and seldom talked openly about the sword of doom that hung over their lives. The problem, Dr. Bermann noted, created terrible tensions that were acted out obliquely on the one son, Roscoe, during his early years. According to Bermann, "With each succeeding visit I began to understand further the depth of the family's trouble. Their terror and desperation of the 'tactics' for avoiding overt recognition of an ever-present death fear became apparent. . . . It became increasingly clear that in the face of their overwhelming dread, this family of seven had—in collusive but entirely nonconscious and unspoken fashion—selected Roscoe as their scapegoat."[7]

In this subtle way the family conspired to make Roscoe the problem. They seldom talked to him or acknowledged his presence. His spirit was broken at home. He conformed when he was at home but on the outside he began to act out his hostility in delinquent ways. According to Bermann, once a child is trained and placed into the scapegoat role, he becomes indispensable to his family. He becomes a target for the family's grievances and, as whipping boy, affects the relationship of different family members to each other.

Roscoe's delinquent behavior began at the age of eight, stemming from his father's physical problem and the family reaction, and continued into his teenage years. He was viewed by society and its helping agencies as a child with a personal problem. In fact, his behavior was a function of the family's structural problems, which stemmed from his father's physical disability. He was arrested more than five times, and his delinquent career was fostered by the further negative socialization of deviance in juvenile detention. It is important to understand a person's family and its sociometric structure in order to understand his or her pathological behavior. In Roscoe's case, his father's illness and the family's reaction obliquely caused his problem.

Severe lifelong physical problems of any member of the family affect the rest of the family emotionally, and most cases of severe physical health problems produce emotional consequences. Despite the enormous negative pressures, in some cases a family successfully coalesces around a member's permanent physical problem—and rises above what might easily become a disaster for the family.

One such case was reported to me in an interview with a professor of social welfare. His intelligent and rational handling of his son's problem serves as a model for the positive management of the lifelong physical and emotional problems that can emerge in a family.

"My son was born with cerebral palsy. By the time he was a year old we had talked to over fifty doctors around the country, including Dr. Spock. No one had any answers or suggestions for our handling the problem that made any sense to me or my wife. I was extremely discouraged. The bottom line was that my son was almost a quadriplegic, with very little movement capability in his arms, legs or head. We weren't sure he would ever walk or talk.

"I went through the usual parental trip connected with such despair. At first we tried to act as if it didn't exist and then we blamed ourselves in some unconscious way. Next we saw it as God's will—but none of these projections helped.

"The most helpful person we met was a pediatrician who said, 'Look, I don't know much more about the problem than you do. But I'm willing to work with you.' We set up long-term and short-term goals for my son, economically, socially and emotionally.

"I became the manager of our therapeutic team, with my wife as my chief aide and the doctor as a consultant. I was fortunate enough to get jobs which enabled me to be home a lot. Our long-term goal was, of course, to get my son to function as normally as possible as a full human being. Our first aim was to get him into a regular public school.

"The school didn't want him at first because they felt he would be a problem, but we talked them into it. My wife and I would take turns pulling him to school on one of these little red wagons that kids have. Once at school we hired some nice sixth-grade kids as 'social prosthetics' who would pick him up and carry him into class. At the end of the school day they would deliver him back to the wagon, and we would then take him home.

"In the meantime, with the pediatrician's help we devised physical exercises to do at home every day to hopefully get him walking. I talked to my son about his feelings a lot when he was a child, and assured him as best I could that we would get him walking and talking properly some day. At that time, in his early years, all he could do was creep, not even crawl, on the floor.

"Yes, we had discipline problems. He would have tantrums and manifest rebellious behavior like other kids. We obviously couldn't and wouldn't spank him. If we had, it would have had negative physical effects on him. If he didn't cooperate and do his daily exercises to strengthen his body, or things like that, I would order him to his room. Sometimes he would say, 'I'm not going!' I would say, 'If I have to carry you, you're there two hours. If you go yourself, it's one hour.' These rational behavioral techniques usually worked.

"We sometimes put candy outside his reach, so he would have to use his physical powers to get to it himself. By the time he was around ten he was attempting to stand. My wife became emotional because the kid would fall down a lot and hurt himself. I felt I had to be tough and rational for his sake. I put a football helmet on his head and knee pads on his knees and told him, 'Fall if you have to, but this is the only way you're going to learn how to walk.' Against the pain of my deepest emotions of 'rach-monas' [Yiddish for 'sympathy'] I had to be tough and rational to help him.

"My own father taught me that by example. During the Great Depression he was out of work and terribly depressed. Finally, he got up one day and got a job. His message to me was: 'How long can I feel bad? God isn't going to help me. I have to help myself.'

184

"During grade school I did what I call contingency role-playing with my son. I call it 'What if?' training. What if, for example, some kid bullies you, or teases you about lying there? In one session I remember we acted out a kid teasing him about not walking. My son developed a self-defensive answer: 'I can't walk, but I can tell time. Would you like me to teach you?'

"By high school my boy could walk with crutches. We would get him to the city bus that went to his school. There a teacher's aid would meet him and get him to his first class. He would then get from class to class on his own."

After the boy finished high school his father decided to advance his own career. He went to New York University and signed up for classes toward his Ph.D. in social psychology. Both father and son went on to complete their doctorates. The son, who is now thirty-eight, is self-sufficient, married, and has a research job with the State of California.

I asked this courageous pragmatic father to delineate the basic principles involved in his helping to create this success story with and for his son.

"As his father I was the supervisor of a rational plan to literally get my son on his feet. I had to control my emotions of pity and self-pity because the kid would then begin to feel that way about himself. With my own father's help I learned to separate the rational from the emotional. This sign on my wall says it all to me." The sign reads: LIFE IS A TRAGEDY OR AN OPPORTUNITY.

The lessons of this case are relevant to all problems, both normal and abnormal, between father and son. Normal crises are opportunities for a father to communicate information to his son, and to show him how to help himself. A loving relationship can be maintained between a father and son in spite of problems.

A level of rational toughness is required in many situations where becoming overly emotional or sympathetic can be a disservice. Another important lesson to be derived from this courageous family situation is that a father can team up with his wife, and in concert they can help solve the most difficult problem. The mother was nurturing, but the father was predominantly responsible for the fact that his son can now function effectively in the real world. Father and mother roles can, of course, be reversed, depending on each parent's strengths.

The father in this case would not accept a projected cognitive map for his son as a cripple. He developed a hopeful plan that ultimately resulted in a victory for both father and son. His rational concern and action serves as an inspiration and a model for all fathers to emulate in their relationships with their sons.

CHAPTER SIX

How to Father: Problems and Solutions

FATHERING A SON is a process that basically involves love and compassion. To recapitulate, each father's approach is basically determined by the style used by his father, the unique social and emotional situation of the man during different phases of his life, the various influences in the family configuration—wife, brothers, sisters—and the basic personality of the father. Another significant dimension in a father's role-playing is the personality of the son, a personality that changes with age and the influence of the growing number of relevant others in his life.

In these contexts a father and son are confronted throughout their relationship with a variety of situations and problems that require solutions. In this chapter I will analyze the basic themes and normal problems that almost always emerge in the various phases of the father-son relationship, and make suggestions for their solution.

In simpler societies where agriculture, hunting or fishing were the main means of sustenance, fathers and sons had a natural, positive and functional relationship. In our more complex, often fragmented, contemporary society, fathers and sons do not relate as naturally or in terms of real functions. Only rarely do they have the opportunity to work together in some occupational situation that they both enjoy.

In our contemporary urban technological society, a son can even be a block to his father's success. A cold-blooded assessment reveals that a son can be costly, time-consuming and demanding. He gets in the way of his father's attempt to devote all of his energies to "making it" in a competitive society.

Because of this, fathers must consciously create situations and conditions which enable them to interact with their sons in quality-time productive circumstances. By "quality time," I mean a situation where a father is almost totally focused on his son, and vice versa.

The more a father and son can overcome the complexity of the contemporary socioeconomic system, which does not produce their natural and functional association, the better. Fathers who are playwrights, truckers, businessmen, politicians or members of any other profession should acquaint their sons with their occupational and recreational worlds, whether or not the sons choose the fathers' occupational paths. The sons, even if they don't follow in their fathers' footsteps, can derive meaningful learning experiences from their fathers when they see them in action in their own settings.

A playwright I know who was relatively distant from his son because of his work habits and lifestyle helped his son acquire a job in a summer stock company. This tuned his son into his father's life work and his position, and gave the two a common area of interest to discuss.

Hunting, fishing, ocean or wilderness activities are natural settings for father and son to relate in—even though these activities do not have the functional meanings they once had for survival. It would be better if a father and son were fishing because they truly needed the fish for food, but being alone together has its intrinsic merits.

Sports activities are also excellent devices for naturally and functionally bringing fathers and sons together. I believe this accounts for the enormous popularity of the little league phenomenon. In this context, it would be valuable to eliminate macho coaches from the game and almost exclusively put fathers and sons into the sport together. It provides a mutual interest they can talk about when they are alone with each other.

Throughout all of my interviews, over 90 percent of my respondents remember their peak experiences with their fathers as occurring when the two of them were alone. Any dilution of the situation by the inclusion of others was viewed with negativity by sons. This desire to get Dad alone in quality time is an emotional hunger felt by almost all sons.

In the process of developing a functional relationship with a son in an artificial society, care should be taken that it is a voluntary participation and not coercive. A father should include his son voluntarily in his occupational and social worlds. The imposition of a particular message or occupational model on the son can kill the son's creativity, spontaneity and the natural flow of his life. Offering possibilities is one thing; the emotional and occupational imprisonment of a son by a father is another.

Forcing a son to fulfill a fixed dream plan of a father is a dismal example of an effort at occupational imprisonment that results in emotional problems for both father and son. In contrast to one with a fixed plan, a father with a more open stance, who is enjoying his own occupation and lifestyle, may find that his son naturally gravitates toward emulating him.

A father is basically a role model to his son. He can be and sometimes is a negative model, who propels his son in the direction opposite to where he would like him to go. As an example of this negative thrust, a son whose father was a professor told me, "We were always poor compared to my friends. There was never enough money. I knew my dad wanted me to get into education. But no way. I recoiled from it. I didn't even want to go to college. He wasn't that happy and fulfilled as a professor, and that turned me off."

In contrast, in an interview I had with an actor, I learned that his two sons had decided to become actors in spite of the fact that he was against it, mainly because he had the usual constant financial struggle that goes with the territory. His dream plan included any profession but acting for his sons. In my interviews with the family I learned that the sons' desire to become actors stemmed from their observation that their father seemed to enjoy his work. For this man acting was fun and a learning experience. He brought a sense of excitement to his work. The sons found their father's joy in his profession contagious, and they wanted to follow in his footsteps, despite the fact that he disapproved.

Some of the playful father-son dynamics in this issue are revealed in the following vignette, told to me by the father. "One day my oldest son, who was then about twenty and had just graduated from college, told me that he really wanted to become a professional actor. I told him about the agony and ecstasy of the profession. I emphasized the agony and the constant difficulties of getting work. The little bastard looked at me and said, 'I know how tough it's been for you, Dad, but for me it's going to be different. I'm going to be a success.' "

Life goals and occupational maps and messages should be wide open and out front between fathers and sons. I recommend periodic discussions between fathers and sons revolving around this subject beginning in the early years. Open communication in private sessions between a father and son early in their relationship can prevent a lot of problems that might otherwise emerge when the son later moves out into the world on his own. At that point sons who have had to work at decoding their fathers' messages may find out that they were wrong about their fathers' hopes for them, and this can lead to a lifelong struggle between father and son. Open and effective communication is crucial. Good communication between a father and his son is the cornerstone to their later desirable man-to-man relationship. When there are communication blocks, fathers and sons should utilize whatever techniques or people are available for helping in eliminating them.

When limited communication exists between a father and son, both parties tend to try to become mind readers of the other's perceptions. In some cases they are right, but they are more apt to be wrong. A young man I interviewed delineated his lifelong communication problem with his father. He revealed a situation that regrettably exists for too many sons and fathers. The father and son suffered for many years before their communication problem was finally resolved through the aid of a priest who was respected by both. The priest was an unusual man who served as go-between and counselor to both father and son. The following extensive case report by the son reveals the kind of unfortunate struggle many other fathers and sons have throughout their lives. More importantly, it demonstrates how a communication block can be eliminated.

"My father is a slightly balding, middle-aged man of fifty. He has been married to my mother for twenty-five years. He is retired from the Navy and holds the rank of chief boatswain. My father and I are very much like one another in our attitudes and actions, to an extent. He is not a very opinionated person, nor does he go out of his way to get involved in matters that are of little importance to him personally. He is a man who stands his ground when he thinks he is right and he does not give in to the stronger party. He is stubborn and he rules his house with an iron hand. He has always believed in very strong, swift and direct discipline for his children.

"This habit my father has of disciplining his children has led to many quarrels and gaps in our family communication in the past. An example of his harsh discipline would be a two-week restriction for a minor offense, such as coming in at one minute past midnight when I was supposed to be in at midnight.

"There were times in my life when I wanted to just run away from home and never come back. Although those times were not everyday occurrences, they added to the total and almost overwhelming need to get out of that place. Because of my father, I almost never spent time at home with the family if I could avoid it. I would never bring my friends home for fear of being berated by my father in front of them for some absurd reason.

"As I got older, my father and I seemed to drift farther and farther apart, to the point of noncommunication. It seemed that we would only talk to each other when we had to, and when the discussion was on a subject of a noninflammatory nature. He was not very disciplinary in my last few years at home, but that was mostly due to my not being around too much.

"Around my senior year in high school, I went on a retreat where I met this great priest. During the retreat he suggested ways of talking to my father to open up communication between us. When I got home I excitedly approached my father and told him that it was time we had a serious talk, because we were not communicating. The following is a brief summation of the conversation.

SON: Dad, I need to talk to you because I think that we are not talking to each other and saying the things that we need to say to each other.

DAD: Go ahead, son. I'm listening.

SON: It bothers me that you and I don't do the things that other kids and their fathers do, like talk to each other, go places, do things and most of all be a father and son.

DAD: Like what? We do things and go places—just last week we all went out to dinner, didn't we? We go to church every Sunday. We have a good family life, don't we?

SON: That's not what I mean, Dad. What I mean is that you and I never talk—

DAD: What do you mean by that? We're talking now, aren't we?

SON: Yeah, but not in a serious tone. It's like it's always been— we talk sometimes, but we don't communicate.

DAD: Communicate? What the hell do you mean by that? You don't even know what you're talking about!

"As usual, after about thirty minutes my father said, 'This conversation is not getting us anywhere.' That was the end of the conversation.

"However, my father and I as a result of that conversation became, I think, somewhat closer to each other in the following days and weeks—at least we were communicating on a more frequent basis and it was not just the 'Hi, how are you doing?' type of communication we had had earlier.

"About two or three months later I sat down with my father again and talked about some things that were on my mind, and like before, when we got into some heavy areas he said that this conversation was 'getting us nowhere fast.' Again, the end of the conversation.

"During the summer months I went on another religious retreat and again talked with the priest about not being able to fully communicate with my dad. He suggested that he should go talk to my dad and maybe he could work something out for us. I was afraid to have him do that because then my dad would get upset at me and say, 'Family business stays in the family, and only in the family.'

"We finally decided that the priest would talk to my father in a roundabout way. And then, if he got a chance, he would bring up the subject of our relationship. Soon the priest, who was quite remarkable, got through to my father, who agreed to have another talk with me. Here is a summary of our three-hour talk.

DAD: Son, there are a lot of reasons for my not talking to you about things and letting you share in my life and they are rather hard to explain. Some of them you may think are irrelevant, but they are a large part of my life.

SON: Go ahead, I'm listening. Take your time.

DAD: Son, when you were younger I saw in you the mirror image of myself. I saw the mistakes I made, the way I acted when I was upset at not being allowed to do something, and other little things that I as a parent now do not approve of. I didn't want you to act that way so I guess I did everything in my power to see that you didn't turn out like me. I guess I overdid it a little. Your mother and I have talked about this before, and I don't know if you noticed it or not, but I have been trying harder to leave you alone and let you run your own life.

SON: I've noticed that you have left me alone, but I thought that it was because you had given up trying to change me, or because you noticed that I was trying to avoid you.

(The father and son are moved by what they have said to each other and they embrace for the first time in many years.)

DAD: Son, now you are almost eighteen. It seems like it was only yesterday that I held you in my arms and thought about how I was going to see to it that you got the world on a silver platter, with no one to bother you because I was going to be there to help you along in life. I used to think of you—and probably still do think of you—as my little boy. The child that I love is no longer a child. This child has grown into a mature young man who no longer needs his father to hold his hand or to tell him what to do or to help him fight his battles. This is very hard for me to accept.

SON: I know, now that I look back on the way you acted, that I can see just how you felt. I just wish that you had come to talk to me about how you really felt, and we could have worked it out. Each of us would have been spared a lot of the pain we've had from each other all these years.

DAD: I just didn't think that you would understand how I felt. I also didn't think we could carry on a conversation without getting into an argument or a fight.

SON: But Dad, all I wanted was a chance to talk to you man-to-man and try to find out what was on your mind, but you always seem to shut the door in my face. Now that you have finally opened up a little, I understand you. I may not understand you all the way, but there is at least some daylight.

DAD: I don't really know how to say this to you, but I just want you to know that I am very proud of you, even if I can't come right out and say it. I'm proud of you and I love you very much.

SON: Dad, I just want you to know how happy I am that after all these years we could just say to each other what needed to be said. I love you too."

According to the son, now twenty-one, "that one conversation where we both expressed our love changed our lives for the better. I talk to my father a lot now, and we really express our feelings."

The son graduated from college and became a probation officer.

It is interesting to note how in this relationship the son misperceived his father for most of his life. He saw his father's style as cold and almost brutal; however, when the father and son broke through each other's emotionally protective shells and truly communicated, they found out how much they loved and cared for each other. There are many fathers who maintain this kind of shell because of a macho style, or a desire to shield their sons from their errors in life.

In my research I found this lifelong communication problem between this father and son mirrored in hundreds of similar cases. Too many fathers and sons have a regrettable lifelong struggle with each other because they misperceive how the other feels in the same way as the father and son I've just described. They don't know how to communicate with each other. Fortunately, the priest who intervened as a surrogate father was able to break down the wall between this father and son and facilitate their communication.

The case described also reveals the needless pain this father and son lived with because of the father's cold, distant, macho style. The man was not a psychopathic or egocentric father. Under his macho-father facade, no doubt fostered by his military orientation, breathed a warm loving-doubling father. Both father and son would have led a happier, more productive earlier life together if this macho father could have discarded his facade and been to his son and family the compassionate, loving man he really was.

A man's father style is best determined by the distance and stance that feels most comfortable to him. An important thing each father should bear in mind is that there is a trade-off of power related to the distance developed between him and his son. The more distant macho father has more control; however, the loving, buddy-type father is apt to have better communication and closeness with his son.

In general, a "close-buddy" father gives a son a kind of loving older brother who is always available for help. This type of father can provide nurturing and emotional support; however, there is often a loss in this type of relationship of authoritative clout when the father's disciplinary role is called for. Buddies can't easily and quickly become the regulatory figure that a father must be when and if his son requires it. Too much familiarity between father and son often produces contempt and insufficient distance for fatherly control.

The more distant macho fathers are more clearly disciplinary agents. Fathers of this type, however, are not as readily available for intimate counseling on subjects such as sexual issues or drug-related behavior. In this distant relationship, a game of "you can't catch me" is played by the son, and the father is often cast in a quasi-detective role.

Some men are almost neuters as fathers. When a father plays an overly distant role on a long-term basis, the mother may try to compensate by becoming both father and mother to the son. As one mother I interviewed told me: "Joel was a terrible father. Not that he did anything wrong with our son—he just didn't do *anything*. The boy saw his father as a nothing. I had to be both father and mother to our son. Why do I think he retreated from being a father? I can only guess that he had had such a bad time with his own father, who was a drunk, that he never learned how to be or even wanted to be a father. He was a good provider and actually a good husband, but a zero as a father."

A father's style, distance and communication are enormously affected by divorce. Since around half the fathers and sons in America live in the shadow of a divorce, it is no minor item as a determining force in the father-son relationship. Even when grounds for the dissolution of a marriage are obvious, the children of divorce experience personal shock. Research on divorce reveals that the children often erroneously feel that they are somehow responsible for the breakup. A divorced father should take great care to let his son know that he is not responsible.

The distance between a father and son created by divorce is an obvious block that must be overcome. The father has enormous obstacles to overcome if he is to be an effective father, especially during Phase I and Phase II of his relationship to his son. Many rational divorced parents work out this problem by allowing the child to live with one parent during Phase I and the other parent during Phase II. A pragmatic solution (which also has its problems) that I would recommend is that the child live with its same-sex parent during the Phase II adolescent years. In the case of a father and son, although the son needs considerable nurturing during his early years, it is vital that he live with his father during his Phase II adolescent years. During that period he especially requires a loving man who is available to him for guidance and as a role model. The son will miss many emotional ingredients because of his father's absence during the early years. However, on balance, if a choice has to be made, he should be with his father during the teenage years.

Another significant factor to be recognized by divorced parents is their role as filter and transmitter of the image of the absentee parent. When the mother has custody she should be extremely careful *not* to inflict her normal hostility toward the absent father onto the male son, who may look and act like his father. Moreover, she should take considerable care *not* to transmit a negative image to him of his now distant father.

Weekend Fathers, a book by Myrna and Jerry Silver, delineates many of the significant issues that exist for the divorced father. The authors, recently married to each other, are both veterans of former twenty-year marriages, and they discuss the issues from personal experience. Jerry, the father of four children, commented as follows about the general problem of the divorced father in the preface to the book:

"Divorced fathers comprise the most oppressed minority in our country, economically, socially and emotionally. . . . In the stampede to help women, men are being trampled. . . . The courts have an entrenched bias toward women gaining custody of the children. The next major revolution must be men's rights. We are not trying to polarize this thing [father's rights], but strike a balance. We're not trying to turn the tables and simply say men have been shabbily treated. We're saying we want the men to get a fair shake. . . ."[1]

Myrna Silver, an ardent feminist, comments on the issue of divorced fathers: "When I started attending meetings of the divorced fathers' rights group. . . . I found a great rage growing in me at the attitude men have toward themselves. They discount their own worth as fathers and human beings. Women have gained all the sympathy and help of men and women all over the country in their struggle for equality. But people still smile disparagingly when we talk about equality for men. I have learned that gentleness, sensitivity, caring, love and the ability to parent know no gender."[2]

Divorced fathers, despite many obstacles, should make a special effort to spend prolonged periods of time with their sons, for example during vacations. Lengthy periods of quality time with their sons provide an opportunity to fulfill the sons' keen feelings of wanting to be alone with their fathers.

Many organizations have emerged to support the divorced father. A father who meets regularly with a group of divorced fathers described some of the issues they deal with.

"The actual raising of a brood of children is still frightening to a man alone. The group has been clumsily confronting problems like how to get a fever down, how to give an enema, where to find milk at six in the morning, how to help sons with bedwetting traumas. A basic problem is the absence of your spouse. Sometimes you'll hear your kid crying in his sleep and you'll go to comfort him. You'll sit there in the middle of the night trying to find the words to explain what happened, why his mother isn't

197

around. I've never had an explanation. I've only been able to hold him and tell him it's going to be okay some day."

My research reveals that after divorced fathers, fathers consumed by their work are next in line when it comes to being distanced from their sons. Workaholic fathers who do not make an active effort to avoid the problem tend to become egocentric fathers. Their usually complex business occupations require inordinate amounts of time in getting and maintaining success and status. They are very apt to be distanced from their sons for extended periods of time and egocentrically involved in their work. This cuts down on the quality time and attention they can give to their sons, unless they make special efforts to circumvent the problem.

Often such work-besieged fathers are overly generous with their sons with material things as a kind of payoff, out of a guilt felt from not spending sufficient quality time with their children. This payoff process may be more prevalent among high-status parents; however, it is a phenomenon that occurs in fathers from all socioeconomic positions. Sons of rich or poor men who are handed rewards (monetary or status) on a silver platter often become failures in their own lives. They do not learn the processes of achievement. They are shielded from the steps involved in earning money and position.

Inundating a son with material things and a status he has not personally earned can be most destructive. The father gives his son things in place of the quality time which the son really needs and wants from his father. The "too much too soon" syndrome can be emotionally crippling because the son has never experienced the processes of learning how to live in society.

A large number of middle-class men and an even greater number of wealthy ones add psychotherapy to their sons' lives in order to dodge the responsibility of fathering their sons. The egocentric father who is success-involved may gladly turn his role over to a therapist, who in effect becomes the son's therapeutic father-surrogate.

There are, of course, many instances where a therapist is needed and functions effectively in reuniting a father and son through the therapeutic process. Dr. Gene Landy, an innovative psychologist, has successfully intervened in such cases in his practice with young adults who have problems with their fathers.[3] His approach involves removing the son from the negative influences of the "too much too soon" situation. He develops a written contract with the father and son whereby for a period of time the therapist takes complete control of the son, including the allocation of any money. The son is then encouraged by the therapist to perform in the real world, learn some of its processes and work for his sustenance. The therapist functions as a back-up support system, and counsels the son on how to handle the various problems that he has difficulty handling on his own. The difficult goal of the process is to reunite the son with his father through making the son less dependent on his father.

A nouveau riche father and his son present a typical problem of this genre. The father has worked hard to get where he is, and the son approaches his inheritance of wealth in a quite matter-of-fact way. The father is a more developed person because he has had to work his way up the ladder. His son doesn't usually understand this process and this can lead to conflict between the two.

The following father-son case that I worked with in group therapy delineates the "too much too soon" syndrome and how it can be resolved.

The thirty-year-old son, Jules, was a college dropout. The problems began when Jules started working in his father's trucking business. He started therapy because when he worked with his father he was constantly fighting with him. As a result of the conflict with his father he became extremely depressed. In an attempt to overcome his depression he began to use cocaine and other mood-elevating drugs. As he put it when he showed up in the group, "I'm drowning in drugs and I want to get off that terrible merry-go-round."

The father began as a poor immigrant from Russia. He started as a driver, and over a period of forty years he built a trucking business into a multimillion-dollar empire. Throughout most of his life, the workaholic father was gone a lot, and overindulged his son with almost every material item that money could buy. All his son had to do was ask, and he would receive. The father had learned the hard way how the world works. His son never learned the process of work and achievement. The son couldn't understand why his father continued to work, since, as he observed in one session, "he has all the money he'll ever need." Their conflict revolved around their work situation with the father and son arguing over the son's lateness and laziness.

Why the two men differed so much in their approach was clear. The father had worked his way up from being a penniless immigrant, and the son acquired his position in the business on the proverbial silver platter. The father's achievements came through dedicated work. The son grew up in a "golden ghetto," with people more involved with spending money than earning it.

After the son had been in my group for a while, I saw him and the father together alone. After a number of sessions with them, during which I explained their problem, the father and son began to communicate and understand the other's point of view. This helped them both to relate to each other more effectively. The son began to listen to his father. In a psychodrama I ran with them, I had them reverse roles. The son in playing the role of the father began to understand more about his viewpoint on life. He learned that his father really loved him deeply and cared about him. For the first time in his life the father began to understand his son's viewpoint on life, and how he had grown up without learning to achieve on his own.

As a result of their deep communication in sessions over a period of a year, they understood each other much better. The son significantly reduced his use of drugs and the father and son became compatible business associates and good friends. They both realized how much they cared for each other.

Another wealthy man who made it the hard way averted the problems described in this case by bringing his son up with a greater sense of reality than Jules. The son in this instance was a graduate student of mine in sociology with whom I had long discussions about the issues involved. He analyzed his father's approach to training him effectively in understanding the ways of the world as follows:

"My father was a poor kid and he climbed the ladder of success the hard way. He never stopped telling me stories about how tough it was for him. He would go into great detail about how he managed to work his way up to where he was now from a very humble position in life. I have to admit that a lot of my father's stories about his working his way up the ladder were boring when he told them to me. But he made me sit and listen to all of his travails and problems, and how he solved them each step of the way.

"When I was a teenager he invented jobs so that I'd earn things the hard way. It was a game, because I knew the gardener could garden better than I, and my father could afford to pay him. Sometimes when he would give me a story about 'earning' my ski trip or a new bike, I would really get pissed off at him. He could have just given me the money. He certainly had it.

"But looking back I'll tell you the truth—I'm grateful to him. Because unlike some of my wealthy friends who had things handed to them, my father taught me something about the value of working for a dollar. A lot of my friends who had things handed to them by their wealthy parents went off on drugs, are still lying around the house, or worse. I'm grateful to my old man.

"I partly earned my way through college, and I have a pretty good idea about how life really is—because he helped me to find out for myself."

Unlike this father, who perceptively introduced realities into his son's life training, egocentric fathers overindulge their sons. Rather than giving them the quality time and fathering they require, the fathers buy them off (usually out of guilt) with money and material objects. The pay-off is for the purpose of keeping the son satiated and it eliminates the responsibility to really father. Fathers who function in this egocentric way may take care of their sons' material needs, but they don't assume their most significant father role, that of illustrating the way the world works to their sons. When the father doesn't take the time to perform this task effectively, a surrogate father in the form of a therapist of some type may have to be called in to handle the resulting problems that arise.

This process of socially educating sons requires much more time, energy and ingenuity than the easier route of material payoffs. I often explain these issues to my own teenage son in this way: "I can give you money and support you fairly well as long as I live. But you may never learn the value of a dollar, or what's involved in working for yourself. Dependent people are slaves to the people they are dependent on. And slaves don't like their masters. When you create your own occupational role in life, are properly independent and earn your own money, you will be a freer, happier person. We can then relate on a man-to-man friendship basis and give to each other."

What all fathers from all positions in life share is the responsibility of educating their sons about the society they live in and how they can effectively earn their own way in life. A father, whatever his style, should not distance himself from his son. He must socialize his son properly by helping him participate directly in life. If he doesn't, his son may experience emotional problems or take dangerous detours into delinquency and drugs when he grows up and has to encounter the real world.

Both rich and successful fathers and poor fathers are confronted with the final act of letting go so their sons can become independent and give to themselves. Sons of poor fathers are more likely to confront life more quickly than the affluent—but all sons must eventually confront life head-on, become independent and self-sufficient.

A father can aid in this process by helping his son to become independent from him as early as possible, and using himself as a visible role model in explaining how the world works. The father should be supportive and on call for advice when it is requested, providing a rescue service for his son only when the situation warrants such action. Through this kind of communication a constructive rather than a destructive relationship can be established between father and son.

Another problem between fathers of all statuses and their sons, one that often requires a solution, is the disparity between some fathers' public images and their images in their sons' eyes. In essence, the father can be seen as a hypocrite by his son. The therapist who is remarkably understanding in counseling his patients but has no time for his son's problems illustrates this kind of hypocrisy. Another example is the educator who never teaches his son what he knows. When there is a disparity between a father's public image and how he treats his son, the disparity intensifies a son's anger toward his father and this creates problems that often result in outright rebellion.

In a case of this type that I was professionally and personally familiar with, the father was an entertainer and a celebrity who was an extraordinary man in his public service. He used his eminence to become an advocate for the oppressed in many significant causes. As a partial result of his many activities and his career, he distanced himself from his son. His son reacted against what he perceived as hypocrisy with a great rage that resulted in severe emotional problems.

His basic problem with his father—and its solution—emerged in a psychodrama session I had with him. He described his great pain in one incident. He was watching a TV show on which his father was the master of ceremonies and chief celebrity fund-raiser for a well-known mental health program. Psychodramatically, the son kicked and broke up the mock TV set (a pillow). He then began to cry and scream at the auxiliary-ego stand-in for his father. "You do all these things for everyone else and you do nothing for me. You're a horrible father. You're a hypocrite. And you're *never* there for me."

In a continuation of the psychodrama he claimed that he dreamed and fantasized killing his father. As is sometimes done in a session, we had him "kill" the auxiliary ego playing the role of his father, and then deliver a eulogy about him—both positive and negative. He chose to "kill" his father with "poison."

In the eulogy he revealed how much he really loved his father and yet how angry he was at him. The anger came from the son's perception of his father as an ideal, humanistic person in the community (which he was), yet a man who in his father role gave very little to his son.

My counseling with the errant father and son produced deeper communication between them. Both of them discussed the father's limitations as a father, and the fact that he didn't give his son enough quality time. He admitted he was a better fund-raiser than a father. The son accepted that it wasn't his fault that his father was not as effective with him as he was in other areas of his life. He did find that his father loved him, wanted to communicate with him more and was trying to improve his fathering skills. There was a rapprochement between the two that helped the son's emotional state. The father kept up his honest communication with his son and cut back on his work. He told his son, "I love you and you're very important to me." The son forgave his father for his past transgressions, and this relieved much of his rage.

Basically this father and son had a communication problem. My therapeutic hypothesis was that the father was obliquely trying to do something about his son's emotional problem by participating in mental health fund-raising drives. He had great difficulty communicating directly with his son. The several psychodrama sessions we had included their reversing roles, and were very helpful to both. The process enabled them to more clearly see each other's point of view, and opened up day-to-day communication.

I have observed in many cases of fathers and sons in all levels in therapy that the opening up of communication between the two is a vital step in finding the solution to their problem. When a father opens up and reveals to his son the real person behind the image he has developed for the world, there is a basis for a better and more honest relationship.

There are many benefits for fathers and sons when they can reveal their true feelings and selves to each other. It enables a son to truly comprehend his basic male role model with greater insight. He becomes aware of the fact that his father has his own problems. The son who erroneously assumes his father never has problems believes that he will never be as great as his father. The son goes through life placing himself in the shadow of the father's unrealistically perfect image. This often results in the many tragedies we witness of great men's sons who, because they feel they will never measure up to the (unreal) perfect qualities of their fathers, turn to drugs, alcohol and sometimes suicide.

Despite many problems, it should be noted that most sons of high-status fathers attain their own high status in the world. The factors of wealth, family connection and training create a high level of aspiration that causes most sons to achieve. Sons who have good relationships with their fathers and see them as honestly participating in worthwhile occupational activities tend to emulate them.

A well-known actor's son who is a successful actor in his own right told me, "I used to go on the set with my father when I was a kid. It looked like hard work, but everyone seemed so turned on to what they were doing, and they all seemed to be having a great time. And my father, unlike a lot of men in the business, loves his work and his family and is a really happy man. I knew way back that being an actor was what I wanted to do with my life."

This son's identification with his father flowed from the fact that they maintained a closeness involving good communication. The father tuned his son into his lifestyle and his work. He talked about his problems and his position in the world openly with his son.

The actor father, whom I'm sure at one time played Shakespeare's Polonius, in response to my question, "To what do you attribute your success as a father?" said: "No gift is greater on the part of the father than giving himself to his son. That is not only giving of one's time, of one's energies, but of one's inner self. You can't just pass time with a son by giving him two hours or four hours or a day, and going through some exercises of life. By 'giving,' I mean working to acquire him as a friend and as a companion, and that's very, very important.

"I think it is extremely important to guard against setting yourself up as an idol, to be honest and truthful. Let your son know your weaknesses and your failures, and recognize you as a human being with human frailties, so he will never experience a massive letdown as a result of a false and unrealistic evaluation of his father. I strongly recommend that a father share his frailties, his trials, tribulations, successes, failures and vulnerability with his son. Let him in on what is going on with yourself, both positively and negatively."

PHASES AND PHASE DISSONANCE

Problems between fathers and sons can be minimized when fathers become aware of the phases of their relationships to their sons. Each phase has its normal problems and solutions. Ego-blending during Phase I is demanding because it tends to occur for most fathers during an early period in their marriages when they are apt to be personally embroiled with their wives and professionally with their occupations. Most fathers in this phase are apt to be young men climbing their occupational ladder of success and defining their marital situations. Despite this, fathers should overcome the old macho, masculine stereotypes, and plunge in emotionally with their sons. Feelings of involvement and caring for their sons stereotypically attributed solely to the mother are naturally felt and should be acted upon. I would recommend that despite the father's other demands on his time he should become involved in the physical care of the child. The direct care of his son's physical needs brings the father into a close emotional relationship with his son.

Fathers who take the time necessary to immerse themselves in this experience and do not shut off their open, loving emotions become more humanistic, feeling people, not only with their sons and wives but in the world at large. In a broader sense, in a society where men become emotionally immersed in their relationships to their sons we have the basis for a more humanistic overall society, because men who take the time to lovingly double with their sons will necessarily become more compassionate people in their overall human relationships.

When a father functions this way early in his relationship to his son, the child clearly has two parents. The child becomes aware of the loving, compassionate and functional nature of both men and women, and this is valuable for his own later personality development. Of course, there are some differences between the sexes in child care determined by the structure and functioning of society. However, if a father behaves in a loving-doubling way, his son is inoculated early in life against being shut off later on, simply because he is a male, from certain emotions and the expression of these emotions. When fathers function in this positive way there is less chance of stereotyping male and female roles in the larger society.

Another benefit to doubling fathers who participate intensively in their sons' early life training is that they can experience

a productive and joyful "second childhood." Many fathers, because they are now in a stronger status position and have more
wisdom, can participate in some of the joyful experiences of
childhood with their sons. The process of reliving his own childhood through doubling with his son gives a father an opportunity
to correct the negative experiences he had in his own childhood
and gain many insights into his own personality.

This second-chance phenomenon was revealed in context in
a psychodrama session I directed. A mother was in great pain
about the fact that her husband, from whom she was divorced,
had been successful in his attempt to acquire custody of their
three-year-old son.

At one point in her denunciation of the auxiliary ego playing
the role of her hated husband, she shouted, "You're taking Mike
away from me now only because your own father left you when
you were three. You don't want him to suffer the pain you had
as a child." In a less heated moment in the session the group
asked the woman to say more about what she meant by that
remark. She calmly commented that her husband wanted the
boy out of compassion, because he had suffered a great deal
from feelings of being abandoned by his own father when his
parents were divorced.

On further reflection about the session, she again admitted
that her ex-husband's motivation stemmed from compassion for
their son, and her hostility toward him was diminished. She
decided that it wasn't that terrible to give up her son to his father,
because the man obviously loved the boy and was not simply
selfishly taking him away.

The session revealed the general truth that fathers do relive
some of their own childhood through their sons. There's nothing
wrong with the process, but fathers should be honest with themselves, be aware of their "second chance" at their own childhood
and properly use this experience. When a father and son are
aware of this meaning of the father's doubling, and that the
father is not exploiting his son for his own emotional needs, it
can lead to a positive experience for the son, the feeling that on
some level he is "giving" something to his father. Fathers, if they
feel it, should somehow communicate to their sons that they are

not totally self-sacrificing people. They should inform him that they experience joy from the relationship. Such communication is good for both father and son.

Another important plus for a father who doubles with his son in Phase I is that when he enters into his later relationship with his son in the more stormy problematic Phase II adolescent years he is more tuned in to his son, and vice versa. Because father and son are close to each other, the son is less likely to be the rebel he almost must become in his normal adolescence in order to individuate. The father and son who have touched, doubled, communicated and related intensely during Phase I can more gracefully move into the normal problems of Phase II because fundamentally they know and love each other. The father's viewpoints on life during the adolescent years will have more meaning to the son, and he will listen more carefully to his father's messages.

The transition from Phase I to Phase II resolves some structural father-son problems and creates others. In Phase I, up to adolescence, there usually is the normal social Oedipal triangle of conflict among father, son and mother. The son usually wants his mother to himself. And fathers in varying degrees, despite the fact that they love their sons, may get into a subtle tug of war for the wife-mother's time and affection. The now "queen mother" has more power in her family and may use her role for her own ends rather than for the harmony of the family.

An awareness of the social Oedipal triangle is the first step toward minimizing its deleterious impacts on the participants. A father who has an awareness of his son's emotional need for his mother and his own temporary jealousy toward his son is not as apt to unconsciously act out against his son. Fathers should be aware that they might unconsciously use their status power for overkill discipline that is not rational.

The mother in the social Oedipal triangle is in a power position since both father and son basically want more of her attention. She should be careful not to use her power in a self-serving fashion. In fact, I recommend that the participants discuss their triangle as openly as possible so that they do not resort to unconscious acts of hostility.

A major Phase II problem between father and son revolves around the disciplinary process. Prior to adolescence sons tend to be more responsive and less hostile when disciplined. In adolescence, however, when the half-man son is attempting to individuate, he is apt to respond to his father's normal efforts at control with hostility and rebellion.

The father, of course, is only doing his job with his son, who is increasingly moving out of "home rule" into confronting and dealing with society's norms. In the adolescent phase of the father-son relationship, the father is naturally called on to assume a law- or norm-enforcement role for the society. He, after all, is a kind of policeman, because part of his job is to instruct his son on the rights and wrongs of behavior in society. This policeman role is inescapable for one of the parents, and it is ordinarily assumed by the father.

The son, at best, can perceive him as a loving policeman. But the son is normally associating with his pals, who are his basic intimates in trying to make some sense of the world of male-female relationships, occupational choices, how to cope with school, the possible uses of various drugs and whether or not this rapidly changing body of his that is feeling sexual urges is good or bad. During this difficult period in life few sons are receptive to their fathers' advice, counsel and especially their discipline. The mother should help in this process by joining forces with the father when he is rationally disciplining his son.

Despite the fact that in almost all prior interactions and phases between father and son there is an element of discipline, education and training by the father of his son, in the adolescent years the son is apt to be more rebellious and resistant to being dominated. He is, after all, becoming a man himself.

A disciplinary response by a father can result from something as simple as cutting classes or as severe as involvement in a delinquent act. In either case the response by the father involves a retaliatory measure, like stopping the son's allowance or, in the case of delinquency, some deprivation of a more severe nature, in an attempt to control the son's behavior.

Some fathers, especially macho fathers, have little difficulty with imposing disciplinary rules and regulations. Others, especially overloving-doubling fathers, are reluctant to inflict what amounts to some level of disciplinary pain on their sons, even when it is obviously logical and in the son's interest that he learn a needed lesson. This inability of a father to discipline his son can become a problem in itself.

The problem may arise out of positive motives by the father. The father who has never moved out of the early doubling phase and remains hooked into his son's pain and joy can't stand seeing his son confronted with some of the painful realities of life. Consequently he ill-advisedly rescues or shields his son from all such matters, which are a natural and important part of the son's ego development.

There are two basic contexts in which discipline occurs, and painful realities must be felt. One is when the father directly imposes a sanction (e.g., no allowance for a week, restrictions on going out, etc.). The father in this instance is in charge of his son's fate in the family.

The second context involves a situation where the son has violated a law of the larger society. The father is not the main disciplinarian, and in many cases may have little power over his son's fate. A father in this type of situation can sometimes rescue his son from the pain of the full impact of the larger society's laws, often to the detriment of his son.

The following case reported to me by an affluent forty-year-old lawyer I interviewed presents some of the main conflicts and issues which affect a father's response to society's disciplining his son.

"Bill was sixteen at the time, doing lots of drugs and getting into trouble. I was constantly rescuing him from being expelled from school for truancy, bad grades—you name it. The final blow came when he was arrested in a department store for shoplifting. He already had a few minor drug arrests on his record, so they brought him to the Beverly Hills police station. On the other charges, before his trial in the juvenile court, he had been released into my custody instead of being taken downtown to the juvenile jail.

"The scene at the police station was the same terrible one I had been through several times. But this time I decided I was not going to rescue him. I'll never forget that painful experience.

After a conversation with my son during which he told me he would never do it again, the juvenile police officer present asked me if I wanted to take him home. I said, 'No, do whatever you do with a case like this.'

"My son looked at me in disbelief. 'Dad, you mean you're going to let them take me to the juvenile jail?' I explained to him as best I could that it would be easier for *me* to take him home, but for his own sake, this time he had to face the real consequences of his behavior. He didn't make it easy on me. He began to beg and cry, 'Dad, don't do this to me.' I told him I wasn't doing anything to him; he had done it to himself.

"He really didn't believe it was happening, nor did I. I vividly remember him looking back at me as they took him away. It was like a bad dream. The next thing I remember I was outside of the police station sitting on the front lawn crying like a baby. People, including cops, came by, asking me if I was okay. I waved them away and kept on sobbing uncontrollably. My crying must have gone on for at least half an hour.

"The sight of a forty-year-old attorney, in a business suit, sitting on the lawn in front of a police station crying must have been something to see. I've reviewed that experience fifty times since in my mind.

"What was I crying about? Was it because I was now the father of a juvenile delinquent? Or was it because of my compassion for my son? Was I crying for him or me? I've since decided it was for both of us."

The family dynamics which produced the son's delinquency were quite complex. However, focusing on this disciplinary event in reviewing the incident with this man, who was a brilliant criminal attorney, we both concluded that the following analysis was accurate. This father had logically decided that it was time for his son to confront in full force the realities and consequences of his accelerating delinquent behavior. If the father rescued his son once again he would be doing him a gross disservice. The act of rescue would be more to assuage the father's feelings than in his son's self-interest. It was painful for the father to let his son go to jail. When he cried he did so out of pity for himself as a father who had admittedly failed and was experiencing the pain of being the father of a delinquent son; and secondly, he was crying out of compassion for the pain his son would experience being in jail.

The experience turned out to be a success story. The son's encounter with the inevitable end-point of his escalating delinquency brought him up short, opened up communication with his father and resulted in a positive change of behavior in the son.

Effective fathering in Phase II often involves biting the bullet and experiencing the personal emotional pain necessary for both father and son to correct dysfunctional behavior. If such behavior is continued, it can be self-destructive for the son, and in its continuing consequences destructive to the father's life as well. When a good father states the old platitude before administering discipline, "This is going to hurt me more than it's going to hurt you," he is often stating a fundamental truth.

A nice-guy approach involving a rescue act for his son may take the father off the hook, but it may be bad for the son. Fathers who do this are not fathering effectively, and have avoided their responsibilities to the detriment of their sons' proper socialization. To protect a child from the consequences of his behavior is to bring him up in an unreal world. At some later time in Phase II of their relationship, a son may thank his father for exposing him to certain realities, as harsh and painful as they might be at the time.

In order to do this correctly, an effective father, in addition to feeling the son's pain when being punished, must bear the brunt of his son's hostility at the moment when he takes a position. In my follow-up session with the father and Bill about a year later, the son told his father:

"Dad, when you let me go off with that cop to jail I truly hated you, and I felt abandoned. But I now understand you did what you had to do. Being locked up in that dump downtown for three days with those really tough kids was an experience I've never forgotten. It made me think about my life. And I decided, never again. I'm glad you did what you did and I thank you."

Many fathers have little difficulty with correct punishment that involves some pain for their sons and themselves. I personally have had great difficulty enforcing discipline on my son because I could not stand seeing him experience any pain. Because

I was not tough enough with him, I feel I did him a disservice. Effective fathering in Phase II often involves the process of letting go and allowing a son to experience the pain and difficulties that result when they misbehave in the real world.

An important facet of this issue is related to determining when a father should help his son, and when it is better to leave him to his own resources and the responses meted out by society. The more he is on his own the better are his chances for developing the techniques necessary for coping with society's responses to his behavior. He can also learn how to work himself out of a bad situation. Individual experiences at this time in his life give him self-confidence and proper independence.

My son's first job at sixteen was part-time work at a hamburger stand. He got the job on his own, which was a real plus. It was *his* job. I was good at reinforcing his motivation by approval; however, I began to make a subtle error. Around a half hour before he was to go to work one day I said, "It's time to go to work, Mitch!"

He rightfully blew up at me. Finally he explained to me, "Dad, it's my job. I'm doing fine. Stay off my back."

My unsolicited help on supervising his promptness was incorrect doubling with a teenager who wanted to succeed on his own terms in his own way. He was right and I was wrong.

Another dimension of the rescuing syndrome is that some sons want to be rescued by their fathers because they do not feel their fathers love them. They perceive being rescued as a sign of love from their fathers. In fact, I have observed that a lot of adolescent deviance is geared not toward rebellion, but instead toward getting a distant, unfeeling father's attention. Sometimes an extreme act is the only way for a son to get his father's attention. Fathers who become aware of this disguised cry for help from their sons should examine the relationship. They are probably not spending enough time with their sons, and not properly communicating their loving feelings. Correcting these two matters can remedy the problems.

The rescuing father should carefully check his motivations. Often his help may be more to gratify his own needs than for the son's benefit. The overloving-doubling father is most apt to be a rescuer. Such fathers should not turn off their empathy for their sons, but they should look at the total situation and determine what is best for their sons and for themselves and their own lives.

During Phase II the rescuer syndrome and overinvolvement with a son may be contraindicated, not only for the benefit of the son but because the father will benefit. Some fathers at this time in their lives may have "had it," meaning that their own personal lives have become unbearably besieged and painful. A father in this situation may rightfully decide at a certain point that his situation of continuing stress must be changed. His own mental health is important and if his son is going to go under in the process of finding himself, so be it. The father has his own life to lead, and the platitude "enough is enough" may be quite valid.

There was a point in my relationship to my son during the stormy Phase II years where I came to the "selfish" and astonishing conclusion that I was entitled to some independence from him and a joyful life of my own. I no longer wanted to empathize with or concern myself excessively with my son's problems. Surprisingly, when I told him this and truly stopped hooking into all his problems and backed off, he began to function more independently and effectively in both school and his personal life. There is a generation gap of ideas and norms that exists during Phase II, and a father who struggles with his son on every issue can be prematurely worn into the ground, sometimes literally.

A father should be aware that he is often a natural enemy when his normal son is trying to individuate. In this phase a teenage son is trying to determine what his own intellectual, athletic and talent strengths are. He has to make many of these discoveries on his own. The father should retreat into a more distant role as an on-call adviser. The model of an emerging nation formerly under colonial rule is applicable here. Emerging nations will not permit their former rulers to meddle too intensively in their affairs. They are, however, very accepting of the help of more mature nations which are not trying to take over but are sincerely and compassionately available to advise them on realistic solutions to their problems. Unsolicited help is suspect, and indeed it is often for the emotional benefit of the "helper" rather than the recipient of help. In Phase II, fathers should be on call rather than on their sons' backs.

A major problem that has to be averted to achieve the desired harmonious man-to-man friendship between a father and son is that of phase dissonance. The dissonance occurs when a father is acting out of synchronization with his father role in a particular phase. One form of phase dissonance that can become a serious problem in both Phases I and II is illustrated by the macho father who prematurely admonishes his child-son to "be a man." Another common Phase II problem occurs when a father continues to overdouble with his teenage son. He should become aware of the fact that his teenage son requires the emotional space to find himself by experimenting with life in order to appropriately separate himself from his father. If the father is still doubling, he is out of synchronization with his son's needs at that time.

It becomes a ludicrous and painful relationship when a father and son are still battling Phase II problems and the son is over twenty years old and should be enjoying a man-to-man Phase III relationship with his father. Some fathers and sons continue their bitter struggle up to the point of the father's death. In some cases the struggle only ends with the father's last act of animosity reflected in his will.

All of these dissonance problems can be averted if both father and son have a maximum awareness of the basic processes that are normal for each phase of their relationship. Harmony can be achieved through the maintenance of relevant, open and meaningful communication between father and son. Positive communication can be maximized if the father delivers a clear philosophical message to his son that is not contaminated by any exorbitant or set-in-cement dreams that he has for his son's role in life.

Relevant others, especially the wife-mother, can foster harmony between a father and son by understanding the phases involved in their relationship. The mother and siblings are important members of the cast involved in the father-son life drama.

If all goes well, a father and son can achieve the desired goal of a harmonious and vital man-to-man friendship. Fathers and sons who become good friends in later years have achieved a relationship that is well worth the struggle. The father's joy in having a friend that he brought into this world, one who loves him and helps him in his later years, is without question worth the effort. The son who develops this ultimate relationship with his father has acquired a lifelong wise friend who knows all about him, loves him and will gladly serve as a helpful counselor to him in all of his life struggles. A son and father who develop and achieve a relationship of this type, one based on love and respect, will both enjoy productive and happy lives in a more harmonious society.

NOTES

CHAPTER ONE
1. Wolff, Geoffrey. *The Duke of Deception*. New York: Random House, 1979, p. 291.
2. Hogbin, H. I. "A New Guinea Childhood." *Oceania*, Vol. 16 (September 1946), p. 275.
3. Friday, Nancy. *My Mother/My Self*. New York: Delacorte Press, 1977, p. 17.
4. *Los Angeles Times*, December 20, 1980, p. 11.

CHAPTER TWO
1. Kronkite, Kathy. *On the Edge of the Spotlight*. New York: Wm. Morrow and Co., 1981, p. 11.
2. Ibid., p. 3.
3. Barrabee, Paul, and Otto Von Mering. "Ethnic Variations in Mental Stress." *Social Problems* (October 1973), pp. 48–53.
4. Stewart, Richard H. *Los Angeles Times*, November 23, 1980, p. 17.
5. For more information on psychodrama, see Yablonsky, Lewis. *Psychodrama*. New York: Gardner Publications, 1981.

CHAPTER THREE
1. Erikson, Erik H. *Childhood and Society*. New York: W. W. Norton and Co., 1963, p. 331.
2. Goldberg, Herb. *The New Male*. New York: Wm. Morrow and Co., 1980, p. 46.
3. Castro, Tony. "Father's New Role: Honoring Thy Son." *Los Angeles Herald Examiner*, October 2, 1980, p. A-3.

CHAPTER FOUR

1. *Los Angeles Herald Examiner*, May 29, 1981, p. A-8.

2. Arkin, William. "Brother as a Male Family Role." *The Family Coordinator* (October 1979), pp. 630–33.

3. Toman, W. "Birth Order Rules All." *Psychology Today* (March 1970), pp. 45–49.

4. Robertiello, Richard. *A Man in the Making*. New York: Richard Marek Publishers, 1979, p. 30.

5. Ibid., p. 31.

6. Ibid., p. 36.

7. Ibid., p. 37.

8. Hetherington, E. Mavis, Martha Cox, and Roger Cox. "Divorced Fathers." *The Family Coordinator* (October 1976), pp. 417–29.

9. Gatley, Richard H., and David Koulack. *The Single Father's Handbook*. New York: Anchor-Doubleday, 1979, p. 46.

CHAPTER FIVE

1. Glueck, Elinore, and Sheldon Glueck. *Unraveling Juvenile Delinquency*. Cambridge: Harvard University Press, 1955, p. 73.

2. Andry, Robert G. *Delinquency and Parental Pathology*. London: Staples Press, 1971, p. 133.

3. Bieber, I. *Homosexuality*. New York: Basic Books, 1962, p. 84.

4. Ibid., p. 118.

5. Miller, Brian. "Gay Fathers and Their Children." *The Family Coordinator* (October 1979), pp. 544–53.

6. Greenfeld, Josh. *A Place for Noah*. New York: Holt, Rinehart and Winston, 1978, pp. 1–3.

7. Bermann, Eric. *Scapegoat*. Ann Arbor: University of Michigan Press, 1973, p. 46.

CHAPTER SIX

1. Silver, Myrna, and Jerry Silver. *Weekend Fathers*. New York: Harper and Row, 1981, p. 8.

2. Ibid., p. 3.

3. Landy, Eugene E., and Arnold Dahlke. "Twenty-four Hour Therapy." Free Foundation Publication (June 1980).